"Caitlin is a masterful storyteller and writer who points everyone she encounters back to God's truth. 7 Days to a Life of Limitless is a book for every single Christian to understand the fundamentals of God's love and heart for His children. This book is sure to provide you with lightbulb moments that will help you go deeper with the One who created you and how to experience the freedom that He gives. I'm so thankful for Caitlin's guidance in my own life and that these words have been documented in this book because He really does want you to live a limitless life!"

Shayla Huber
Author of *10 Things I Hate About My Husband*

"This book is so full of wisdom and insight. I love how Caitlin uses analogies in her own life to explain how God works. It helps the reader to understand difficult concepts that might be confusing. She is a true storyteller with a sense of humor! This book gave me so many revelations while reading it."

Alicia Cummings
Author of *Better Days After a Toxic Relationship*

7 Days to a Life of Limitless

How to ditch the rules of religion & discover unrestricted freedom

Caitlin Childs

Book Cover by Shelby Walls

IBSN: (Paperback) 979-8-9896048-0-7

IBSN: (E-book) 979-8-9896048-1-4

CONTENTS

DEDICATION

To my fifth grade teacher, Mrs. Dickerson
You stopped me on the playground and told me that I would
become an author some day.
Your words have been ringing in my ears ever since.

FORWARD

Dear Friend,

    I wrote this book for you. I empathize with your hunger for God and your desire to focus on cultivating a deeper relationship with Him. It seems daunting at times, doesn't it? As if there are too many factors to consider, too many ways you could mess it up. That's exactly why I want you to read these words. I was right there in your shoes. I felt as if I was trying to walk the tightrope of religion, making sure to follow each and every rule so that I didn't disappoint the very Father whose approval I wanted so badly. I just wanted to do the right thing and I'm guessing you do, too.

    Thankfully, the gospel isn't complicated. Religion is complicated; the gospel is simple. Do you believe in Jesus? Do you believe that He died on the cross in order to pave the way for you to be able to have an eternal relationship with your Father? Do you want Him to take His rightful place in the driver's seat of your life so that you can relax a little while He steers you in the right direction? If you answered yes to all of those questions, then you are already considered righteous in His sight. Philippians 3:9 (NLT) says, "I no longer count on my own righteousness through obeying the law; rather, I become righteous through faith in Christ." Did you catch that? Your righteousness does not depend on what you do, it depends on *whose* you are. So let's ditch the rules of religion and start exploring what it looks like to live life as one of God's kids, deal?

I want to preface this book by saying that this is not a book of theology, because I'm still learning as I go. This is also not a "do-as-I-do" instruction manual. This book is simply designed to get you at least one step closer to your Father by sharing the lessons that He has taught me along my path. I know so many people who have struggled with feeling like their relationship with God was "flat" or "uneventful." They wonder if there is more to life than this (because there is). If you're anything like I was, you may even think that your relationship with God is perfectly fine, not even realizing the amount of potential you're missing out on. Honestly, the life I lived before this seems like a fuzzy dream state now. The life I'm currently living feels like I am fully awake and fully alive. All I want is to show you that the same is available to you. Would you allow me that courtesy?

One last thing: I know this may not be easy for you. I realize that you may feel all alone, like you're risking everything to pursue Jesus. I just want to encourage you that if no one else is there to cheer you on, I am. Jesus is. And speaking as someone who is on the other side of this, I can promise you with every breath in me that it is well worth it. You can do this, friend. I'm rooting for you.

Your friend,
Caitlin

—— ◆ ——

INTRODUCTION

It all started with a vision.

I was standing in a horse corral. Something told me that I had been in there for a very, very long time. It was small, but it was comfortable to me; safe, even. Suddenly, the fence dropped. You would think that one would feel an immediate sense of relief and freedom. Not me. I felt an immediate and overwhelming sense of panic. "Where are my boundaries?!" I began to shout, terrified to move. After some time, I put my hands out and started groping at the air as one would do when searching for a lightswitch in the dark. Surely, this is some kind of sick joke. *There's going to be an electric fence or something that's going to zap me at any given moment,* I thought. As I'm pawing at the air and inching my way forward, I catch a glimpse of a figure standing at a short distance to my right. I look over and see Jesus watching me with tears in His eyes.

"I know," He said, "Freedom is hard when you've been trapped inside a cage your whole life."

"Where are my boundaries?" I replied.

"You have none," was His answer.

It wasn't the answer I wanted to hear. This space was too big, too expansive, too intimidating to navigate without some sort of guide-line. *Surely, He can't mean that,* I thought to myself. Right on cue, as if He were responding directly to my thoughts, He spoke. "You have dangers to avoid, such as not jumping off a cliff or diving head first into a rushing river. Other than that, you have the freedom to explore." My eyes wandered to the expansive territory in front of me. Mountains and rivers, fields and forests. How was I to explore this? Where would I even begin?

I found myself desperately aching for the comfort of my corral that I had been in just moments ago. A part of me wanted to go back, pick up the pieces, and build a fence to keep myself in for the rest of my days. But a larger part of me—my sense of wonder and adventure—wouldn't let me. *There's no turning back now,* I thought. *I have to see this through.* "I will be with you every step of the way," I heard.

And so began my journey into limitlessness that God has had in store for me from the foundation of my life. You see, I used to think that following Jesus meant following rules. And for a rule-follower like me, I was fine with that. I felt like the rules kept me safe, when, in reality, Jesus was showing me that these rules kept me stuck. They kept me from exploring all that He had for me. Through this vision, he revealed to me that those "rules" I had been following were really just guidelines to keep me safe while I explored the expansive freedom that He had died to give me.

Over the past few years, He's been taking me on this life-altering adventure of exploring everything that is available to me in this lifetime with Him by my side. I'm beginning to learn just how much there is available to His children and, to be honest, it made me quite angry that the enemy had kept me from discovering the potential that was available to me for so long. The more I explore, the more I hunger for more.

I'd like to take you on that same adventure, to show you which steps I took that led me to where I am today. And I just know that there is going to be someone reading this who truly believes that this particular journey could never be for them. You are the very person I am writing this book for. Trust me when I say that I was fully content to stay inside that cage for the rest of my life. I knew nothing different and I didn't even know that more was available to me until Jesus dropped that fence and set me free. All I'm asking is that you grant me the opportunity to show you that He can do the same for you.

The thing is, this is your life. You have been handed the incredible gift of free will which means that you have the right to choose. Will you stay inside your cage, where you feel comfortable, safe, and small? Or will you take that scary, bold step into the limitless potential that's laid out in front of you?

I thought so. Let's explore.

Over the next seven days, I want to take you on a journey to discover the same limitless life that God placed in front of me the day He gave me that vision. Now, I do want to point out that each of these days will just be an introduction to a new lesson. You'll still need to marinate on them and implement them into your life in order to see growth. Think of this book like me handing you a new puppy. I may have given you the puppy, but you will still need to care for it, nurture it, and give it what it needs in order to keep growing. It's not going to be house-trained overnight. Neither will these lessons transform your life instantaneously. I don't want you to expect your life to be radically altered within seven days because this is not a shortcut to the top of some spiritual mountain. However, by the end of these seven days, I do believe you will be equipped with the tools you need to get there.

I will warn you though, once you begin to implement these things with an honest heart, you will begin to see changes and shifts happening in your life. Not all of them will be fun. At times, the ride will get pretty bumpy and you may even have times where you question God and His goodness. Let me reassure you that that is perfectly normal. I think everyone who is truly striving to get to know the Lord is going to have times where they struggle to understand Him and the way He works. If we never questioned anything, then we wouldn't have a relationship, we would have a religion, or, if we're not careful, even a cult. When (not if) those times come, just remember these words: the truth doesn't mind being questioned, lies do. Jesus is the way, the truth, and the life (John 14:6). As my mom would say, "He's a big boy. He can handle your emotions and your questions, just bring them to Him." Remember the lessons that you will learn throughout this book and continue to press into Him. You're not doing anything wrong when those hard times happen, you're just learning.

For this particular journey, the idea is for you to read one chapter per day so that you can really concentrate on what you're reading and not be overwhelmed with information. Although, nobody is suggesting that those days have to be consecutive. Feel free to pause and ponder as much as you need to. There is a lot of meat in this book. Rather than treating it like a buffet where you fill your plate, eat it all at once and make yourself sick, I want you to treat it like a seven course meal. Give yourself time to digest between each course. We will start with the appetizers that serve as the building blocks for your relationship with Jesus. These are the things that will whet your appetite and make you excited for what's next. Then, we will get to the meat and potatoes of your relationship with God along with answering some of the biggest questions you may be asking like who you are or what you're even doing here in the first place. Finally, we will finish off with dessert. The final chapters in this book will be the sweet parts that wrap everything in a neat little bow. My goal is that you finish this book feeling satisfied with a newfound sense of fulfillment and adventure rather than more questions. Just remember that this is only one meal. And while I hope it's a really good meal, you'll still need to eat again. Don't let your pursuit of Jesus end here. Continue to seek Him by filling yourself with His word and His character, letting Him guide you as far as He wants to take you.

My guess is that if you're picking this book up, you feel like there is way more out there for you than the way you're currently living. Good news! You're absolutely right. And I want to be the one to introduce you to that. By the time you've finished this book, I believe that you will have discovered the key to unlocking what God has for your life. Spoiler alert: Our God is massive, and while He is in the details, He doesn't play small when it comes to blessing His kids. I will warn you, though. The journey won't always be easy. There will be past pains you'll have to face, obstacles to overcome, and opposition to tackle, but when we're talking about living a limitless life, I think that's worth it, don't you?

1

——— ※ ———

HEARING GOD'S VOICE

One comment that I hear most often is, "I wish God would talk to me like He talks to you." Let me just tell you; every time I hear that comment, it releases a deep sadness that oozes into every muscle in my body. People who make those comments have absolutely no idea what is available to them. And because of that, they're sitting on a treasure chest full of untapped potential with no earthly idea of how to find the key.

Allow me to encourage you for a minute and speak some truth into those dreams of yours that are collecting dust on the highest shelf of your mind. God does want to speak to you. Do you believe that? He wants a relationship with you so badly that He sent His only son to earth to be brutally tortured and murdered just to give you the option of having a relationship with Him. And yet, we seem to think that our potential with Him ends right there. Where did we get the idea that accepting the gift of salvation is the most God has to offer us in this lifetime? When did we pick up the notion that a close, intimate relationship with Him is only reserved for missionaries and pastors and is not available to "normal people" like you and me? I'm here to tell you right now that those ideas are bogus. They are completely fabricated lies from the pits of hell designed to keep you stuck. Because if Satan can't keep you from getting saved, his next best strategy is to keep you from unlocking everything that God has for you and bringing a whole lot more people to heaven with you along the way. You see, the enemy likes to play teeter-totter with all of us. He simultaneously tells us that we're too much and not enough. If you start to drift one way or another, all he has to do is make one little comment to keep you stuck between a rock and a hard place for the rest of your life.

Doesn't that make you mad? Doesn't that make you feel like a puppet who's being used for someone else's agenda? I'll tell you, when I had that revelation, it made my stomach churn. But there is good news. The Son of God came to set you free. He wants to set you free from the chains that the enemy has strapped around your wrists and then tries to convince you that they don't exist. Once you realize that, there is a whole world of hope at your fingertips just waiting for you to explore it. That's why John 8:36 says, "So if the Son sets you free, you will be free indeed." So, let me ask you: Are you ready to be free?

Maybe you feel like you don't deserve to have a relationship with Him. Maybe you feel like He's been silent throughout your life because He must be angry with you for all of the less-than-perfect things you've done. Sure, you've done your best most of the time, but you still fall short. You do realize that's normal, right? I'm sure you've heard the verse "For all have sinned and fall short of the glory of God." Romans 3:23. Did you know that's only half of the verse? Have you ever heard the rest? "And all are justified freely by his grace through the redemption that came by Christ Jesus." You see, because Jesus died on the cross for you, that standard of perfection has been dropped. The new standard can be found in John 3:16, "For God so loved the world that He gave His one and only Son, that whoever believes in him shall not perish but have eternal life." If you accept Jesus as your Lord and Savior and believe that He died on the cross for your sins, you've already achieved the new standard of righteousness. Yes, it's that simple.

Allow me to drive this point home by sharing with you one of the things God taught me through one of our earlier conversations. I was watching TV one night and felt Him nudge me to turn it off so that He could talk to me. I obeyed. "I want to talk to you about what you earn versus what you deserve," He said, "Why don't you tell me the kind of things that you earn?" I thought for a minute and replied, "Well, I guess you could earn money, you could earn people's trust, you could earn people's respect." "Yes," He answered, "Now what do you deserve?" Now, I don't know about you, but I had been in Sunday school all of my life. I knew this answer. I very confidently said, "Nothing. I deserve nothing because I'm a dirty, dirty sinner and apart from you, I am worthless." I sat back in my chair, smiling, feeling as though I had just passed some sort of test. Imagine my surprise when He answered, "Wrong. That was the old you that was separated from me through sin. You're a new creation now, so what you deserve is everything that I paid for with my Son on the cross." Whew! I felt like I had just been hit with a jolt of electricity. What a wake-up call. He continued, "You are royalty. You're a daughter of The King. Daughters of kings don't earn their title. It is given to them simply because of who their father is. It is their birthright." Those few sentences shifted my entire perspective on the way that I related to my heavenly Father. I learned that I don't have to approach Him as some lowly, worthless servant groveling at His feet. I'm expected to approach Him as His daughter, with all of the love and authority that is attached to that title. I want you to begin to approach Him the same way.

In addition to approaching Him as a child, I also want you to approach Him with expectancy. Remove the words "I can't hear God's voice" from your vocabulary. Hearing Him takes faith that He will speak to you. If you think you won't hear anything, then you won't be listening. You remember the story of the fishermen, don't you (Luke 5 and John 21)? The one where they had been out fishing all night and hadn't caught anything. Suddenly, Jesus shows up on the scene and asks them to go back out and throw out their nets again. They very easily could have said, "No way. We won't catch anything. I know because I've already tried." It took faith for them to be willing to get back out there and try again. That faith paid off when they hauled in so much fish that their nets were breaking.

> IF YOU DON'T PUT YOUR NET INTO THE WATER, YOU WON'T
> CATCH ANY FISH.

Just because you've tried to hear Him before and didn't hear His voice doesn't mean you never will. You just have to have the courage to try again.

HOW TO HEAR HIS VOICE

The first thing that I tell people when they say that they want a deeper relationship with God is that you need to learn to hear His voice. My mom taught me how to do this when I was a teenager, and I still consider it to be the most fundamental part of my faith to date. I've experienced miracles and had radical encounters with God, but if I were unable to hear His voice, I think I would probably feel a lot like a sailboat without a sail, just drifting through life hoping I end up somewhere nice. Once you're able to hear His voice for yourself, you begin to develop a sense of direction. You'll notice that He begins to gently guide you and teach you as you move about your journey. You still may not know exactly where you're headed, but you'll know what direction you're going. There's a sense of divine purpose attached to the ability to hear His voice.

> THERE'S A SENSE OF RELIEF THAT COMES WITH KNOWING THAT HE IS STEERING THE SHIP AND YOU NO LONGER HAVE TO REMAIN ADRIFT.

At times, I've seen people shy away from the pursuit of God's voice because they feel as though they have to get their ducks in a row first. Let me assure you that you are completely free to come as you are. You don't have to stop sinning, read your Bible, fix your relationships, or join a church before you're able to come to Jesus. Our idea of the way relationships should be set up has kind of warped our idea of how we interact with God. We think that we have to know Him super well before He interacts with us, kind of like how we think that we have to date someone for a while before they'll propose. What we're forgetting is that God already knows everything there is to know about us. In Jeremiah 1:5 God says, "Before I formed you in the womb, I knew you." In fact, the Bible also says that God's thoughts about us outnumber the grains of sand. (Psalms 139: 17-18). Whoa. I would think that someone who thinks about me that often is already in love with me.

> YOU DON'T HAVE TO CONVINCE GOD TO FALL IN LOVE WITH
> YOU, HE'S ALREADY THERE.

Despite your flaws, despite your shortcomings, the maker of the universe is absolutely obsessed with you. All He wants you to do is come to Him and allow Him to show you that.

James 1:5 says, "If any of you lacks wisdom, you should ask God, who gives generously to all without finding fault, and it will be given to you." Before you do anything, I would encourage you to ask God to reveal Himself to you. Our Father wants to be known by His children, and He's not going to withhold Himself from you if you diligently seek Him. Sometimes it just takes a little practice. I want to introduce you to the exercise that honed my ability to hear from my heavenly Father. You're going to need a notebook or some loose leaf paper and two different colored ink pens. In the first color, I want you to write out your prayers to God. And I mean really pour your heart out. Get raw and get honest. Bring Him your troubles, your worries, your thoughts and your emotions. "Cast all of your anxiety on Him because He cares for you." 1 Peter 5:7. Once you feel like you've gotten to a stopping point, switch ink pens. Then you're going to sit and listen. You're going to wait until a thought pops into your mind and you're going to write it down. Even if you think it's your own thoughts, just write it down. Keep writing and listening until you feel satisfied with the response to your prayers.

By this point, you should have two pretty lengthy entries, so it's time to start separating your voice from God's voice. This is where I want to step in and remind you that hearing God's voice takes practice and you're not going to get it overnight, so I don't want you to get discouraged.

I once heard a story about a woman who was a speech and language pathologist.[1] She often worked with children who had cochlear implants. On the days where she would turn on the implants so that these children could hear their parent's voices for the first time, she said she noticed a pattern. The parents would often speak the same two things over each of these children. First, they would say their name, and then they would tell the child they loved them. Identity and love. Isn't that what all of us want to be spoken into our lives? I can confirm to you that the first time I heard God's voice, He communicated similar things. He spoke about my identity, and He told me how much I was loved. However, if you have a strong sense of identity already, He may communicate to you more about who He is. Regardless, He always speaks love. Keep an ear out for statements with undertones of love.

In the story I just mentioned, this woman said that while hearing their parents' voices for the first time was wonderful, these kids still had a lot of progress to make. According to her, children with cochlear implants struggle to distinguish between noises right away. So a knock at the door may sound very similar to a dog barking. They had to spend hours and hours training their ears and their brains to differentiate the sounds they were hearing. It's no different than learning to hear God's voice. It's going to take practice. You're going to have to put in the time to "fine tune your ear" so to speak.

I realize that this exercise may make you feel a little silly at first. The enemy will try to convince you that you're crazy, that you're only hearing your own thoughts or that you're not special enough or perfect enough to have a conversation with God. Good thing we've already debunked that approach. The Bible says in John 10:27 (KJV), "My sheep hear my voice." If you are allowing God to shepherd you through this life, that makes you one of His sheep. You can hear Him. Nowhere in that passage does it say "They might hear me," or

"They usually hear me." It says that His sheep *do* hear Him. The only reason why you believe that you can't is because there is a very real enemy trying his best to keep you from your Father. Don't let him win. If Satan can get away with it, he'll even have you questioning if God is real. The Truth doesn't mind being questioned, remember? You have nothing to lose and everything to learn. Push through the awkwardness until you get to a point where your pages are filled with both questions and answers.

Once you've got your completed journal entry, along with what you believe was the response, how do you know if it was God's voice or not? The first time I did this, I sat down with my mom and we went over the entries. She helped me compare the responses to scripture to see if what I heard aligned with God's word and His character. As we sat at that dining room table, she would take a statement I had written down and flip through her worn out Bible to find verses that correlated and confirmed what I had heard. If you have a trusted friend or mentor in your life that knows their Bible a little better than you do and has a little more experience with hearing God's voice, this may be a good time to ask them to help you. This takes vulnerability on your part, letting someone else examine the words that are written on your raw heart, but real community is built on the foundation of vulnerability. Don't be ashamed or embarrassed. That's exactly where the enemy wants you and we don't let him win, remember?

However, if you feel like you don't possibly have a single person in your life who can help you work through this exercise, that doesn't mean your situation is hopeless. That's what the internet is for. Pray over your journal entry and ask God to reveal Himself to you. Then start to do an internet search for Bible verses that correlate with certain keywords or phrases from your entry. Whenever you find one that lines up with what you've written, you will have no doubt that the

Holy Spirit is speaking to you through those words. Those moments kind of feel like you've just unearthed some hidden treasure. It's a feeling of discovery.

WHAT HIS VOICE SOUNDS LIKE

So what does His voice actually sound like? I believe this can be different things for different people. I've found that God is extremely intimate. He will often customize our experiences with Him according to our unique personalities. For example, I am a highly creative, highly visual person. I believe that's why He often gives me images or visions that I see with my mind's eye. Think of it kind of like a movie playing in your head, almost like a daydream, except you're not in charge of the movie that's playing. He also speaks to me through metaphors, stories, and analogies because that's the way that my brain best makes sense of things. You will most likely find that your relationship with Him is custom tailored to your personality. That's just how relational He is with His children.

Now, when I say that I hear His voice, I want you to understand that I'm not hearing an audible voice whispering in my ear from the great beyond. It's more like a thought that pops into your mind, except you begin to distinguish which thoughts are coming from you and which aren't. Sometimes He will use words or phrases that I would not use myself. Other times, instead of giving me an outright answer to a question that I've asked Him, He will give me a question in response in order to make me think. I know that that's God, because there's no way that I could think of the right questions to ask myself in order to help myself come to the right conclusion. If I were able to do that, I'd probably be labeled an absolute genius and, I promise you, I'm not that smart.

As time goes on, you will start to discover the unique way in which God communicates with you. As you do, it's important to keep in mind that if it is truly God speaking to you, His voice will never contradict scripture. So if you're unsure if what you're hearing is actually biblical or not, just ask Him to give you a scripture to back up what you're hearing. Remember, the truth doesn't mind being questioned because it has nothing to hide. If you're not familiar enough with scripture to have anything brought to your memory, it's time to start reading, my friend. You cannot rely on what you believe to be the voice of God alone. That is dangerous territory and a breeding ground for the enemy's schemes. We don't let the enemy win, remember? And if we're not going to let him win, we need to have a good defensive strategy against the tricks he tries to pull.

WHAT HIS VOICE DOESN'T SOUND LIKE

Speaking of the enemy, let's chat for a minute about what God's voice doesn't sound like. Boy, I could go on a whole rant with this subject, mostly because I felt like I was lied to for so long. I used to have this mean little voice inside my head who told me all kinds of awful things about myself, about what others thought of me, and about what God thought of me. I just thought that that mean little voice was my own thoughts. I thought that that's what the voice inside everyone's head sounded like right up until the moment God delivered me from that spirit of deception.

If you question whether or not God can speak to you through your thoughts, let me ask you this. Have you ever had an intrusive thought? You know, one of those thoughts that pop into your head that are so horrible you can't even believe you would think that? I sure hope you're aware that those thoughts aren't coming from you. And if those thoughts aren't coming from you, that means they must be coming from an outside source. God would never give you thoughts like that so deductive reasoning would lead us to assume that that source would be the enemy and his legion of gremlins, right? So if the enemy can send you a laundry list of intrusive, destructive, and hateful thoughts throughout the day, what leads you to believe that the almighty God that we serve would never dare enter the battlefield of your mind?

Let me tell you something, my friend.

GOD'S VOICE WILL NEVER EVER BRING SHAME, GUILT, CONDEMNATION, OR REJECTION. GOD'S VOICE GROUNDS US, IT'S OUR OWN THOUGHTS THAT MAKE US SPIRAL.

At worst, His voice will bring forth repentance, which is actually a very good thing. If you don't understand the difference, allow me to explain.

We recently adopted some equine. At the time of this writing, we currently have a donkey, a mule, and a horse. Since we had never had these types of animals before, there were a few things I had to explain to my children. I taught them about how it's important to never approach these animals from behind because if they get spooked, they could kick and injure my child. We've also talked about being careful not to get under their feet and how to properly hold treats in their hands so their fingers don't get bit. As I was explaining these things to my kids, I was doing it in a way so that they understood these rules were for their protection and their benefit, which made them want to listen and obey them. I was not yelling at them and making them feel stupid for not knowing this information that they never could've known on their own without my help. I also wasn't trying to give them a bunch of rules to prevent them from feeling like they could interact with the animals at all. Do you see the difference?

You know how the Bible says we're supposed to take all of our thoughts captive and make them obedient to Christ (2 Corinthians 10:5)? Learning to hear God's voice is a prime example of that. Each time a thought enters your mind, I want you to snatch it right out of thin air as if you're grabbing at one of those pesky fruit flies. Take it and examine it. Is this mean, hateful, disturbing, or anxiety-inducing? Chances are that's the enemy. Is it loving, uplifting, gracious, and kind? Chances are that's your Father. Is it in line with what I'm currently wanting or hoping for? It could be God, or it could be you. As time goes on, you will be able to tell the difference.

WHEN GOD IS SILENT

Inevitably, there will be times in your spiritual walk where God will go quiet. Before you start spiraling down the rabbit hole of all of the things you could've done wrong to cause this distance, I want to point out a few reasons why God intentionally goes quiet on us. Yes, sometimes it's a strategy of His in order to work things together for our good.

I was standing in my kitchen one day when God gave me a vision. There was a person trying to follow Him, but they had a blindfold on. They couldn't see Him, they could only hear His voice. He was standing right in front of them saying, "Come to me. I'm right here." The person would take a step forward and God would take a step back, moving in sync with them. "Come to me, I'm right here," He would repeat. They kept moving this way until God took a step back without saying anything. This time, instead of taking a step forward, the person reached out their arms in search of Him. As they did, they discovered that He was still right there, with them the entire time. Those steps that He was taking away from them wasn't to create distance between them, it was to lead them toward their destiny.

> **IF WE'RE WILLING TO PRESS IN AND FOLLOW HIM EVEN WHEN HE GOES SILENT, FINDING OUR DESTINY IS INEVITABLE.**

Sometimes, God will instruct us with His voice. He will tell us which direction to move in in order to find Him. Other times, He goes silent. One of the reasons why I believe He does this is because He wants us to reach for Him, to remember that we are dependent on Him to guide us and so that we don't get too comfortable in our own ability to carry out the steps He's having us take.

Another reason that He might go silent is because He doesn't want us to believe that we always have to be doing something to please Him. We will talk about rest a little bit later and why that is so important in our walk with Him. In order to have a well-rounded relationship with Him, we have to have breaks built in. And if we aren't willing to take these breaks ourselves, you can guarantee that His silence will forcefully bring you to a halt. Think about little children attending school. They are learning more information than their brains have ever taken in before. Because of that, there are scheduled times for them to rest, play, and participate in other activities. God designed our bodies and He knows exactly what we need when we need it. When He goes silent, you may want to take that as an indication that it's time to shift gears in one form or another.

As I began writing this book, I had an entire season where it felt like God was way more silent than He normally is with me. It made me very uncomfortable, and it made me miss all of those times when He was so close that I could practically feel Him. I knew that I was doing exactly what He asked me to do, and that I couldn't possibly have done anything wrong to cause Him to withdraw. I knew that wasn't in His character.

After I finished my first draft, my family took time to spend a day at the lake. There was a beautiful sandbar where the kids could splash in the water. As my husband was standing with my children, I walked about 20 feet away to a sunny patch of grass where I could lay my towel down and tan my skin. As I sat there watching my children interact with each other, I heard God speak to me. "This is what I'm doing with you. You think I've left, when really I'm just a few feet away. I can still hear you and see you, but I'm giving you the space to learn how to trust yourself as you accomplish this task I've given you. I'm still right here, I'm just enjoying watching you become more independent." See, I used to think that I needed to ask God's permission for every single solitary thing I did. And while my intentions were pure, that was stifling my growth like a child who refuses to walk unless they're holding their parent's hand. That day, He gave me permission to act on my own and make decisions on my own because I had learned enough about Him to know whether or not I was in line with what He had called me to do. I said, "God, I thought you wanted me to be dependent on you for everything. How can I do that if you're telling me I don't need to ask your permission all of the time?" His response was, "Dependent, yes. Not codependent." Yikes. Because I had spent so much time seeking His validation for the choices I was making, I had stepped into the old habit of finding my worth in approval. As our Father, God wants to empower and uplift us. With time, you'll learn that while He's teaching us how to trust Him, He's also teaching us how to trust ourselves.

My son is currently five years old. His sister just turned two. Because of her age, she still needs me to do a lot of things for her, and because of his age, I'm expecting my son to do more and more on his own. At first, he was hurt by that. He was upset that his sister seemed to be getting the most amount of attention. Until one day, I flipped the situation on its head. I started praising my son for all of the things he was able to accomplish by himself. Whenever he was in earshot, I would say things to his sister like, "Your brother is such a big boy for getting himself dressed. One day, you're going to be able to do that all by yourself too!" My goal was to help him see that maturing is the goal. Of course, we still need to follow God's guidance, but if I ask my son to get himself dressed, I'm expecting him to do so without asking for my approval for each and every article of clothing he picks out. So long as you are in line with what God has instructed you to do (either through His spoken or written word), then you do not need to ask His permission for every single solitary thing. That's called codependency, and that is not what we're aiming for.

WHEN YOU HEAR HIM WRONG

There's one last thing I want to leave you with for the day. As you set out on this pathway of discovering God's voice, there are going to be times when you get it wrong, and that's okay.

> GOD'S NOT GOING TO SMITE YOU FOR PURSUING HIM IN-CORRECTLY.

Think of it like hearing the lyrics of a song incorrectly. When I was younger, there was this country song that used to come on the radio called "That's What I Love About Sunday."[2] Towards the end of the song, there is a line that says, "New believers getting baptized." But for the longest time, I thought it said, "Little Ebert's getting baptized." I would belt that song at the top of my lungs every time it came on the radio until one day my older brother laughingly pointed out that those were not the right lyrics. However, in my mind, the way I sang it made sense to me. Throughout the song, it listed specific people. "Raymond's in his Sunday best," "There's the Martin's walking in," "sweet Miss Betty likes to sing off key." It only made sense that there would be a sweet little Ebert in this story. But alas, Ebert was a figment of my imagination; something I had concocted all on my own. And yet, when I got the lyrics wrong, nobody made me feel bad about it. In fact, it became a hilarious joke that the entire family still talks about decades later. I'd like to think that God approaches our mistakes with the same amount of humor. Trust me, He's just glad you're trying.

2

⸺ ◦ ⸺

PROMISES

Learning how to hear God's voice is a great foundation, but the promises of God that are specific to your life are what keep you tethered to the future. They are what encourage you to keep going when nothing around you feels firm enough to stand on. You can *always* stand on the promises of God.

I once asked God to explain to me how He exists outside of time. I wanted Him to break it down for me like I was five years old. Immediately, He gave me a vision of Himself standing in a massive library. Think of the library in *Beauty and The Beast*. There were more books than anyone could ever read, lining the walls in a room that had to be at least two stories high. He explained to me that each book represented a person's life. He said that He could pick up any book and flip to any chapter and read any page He wanted, whenever He wanted. "One thing I want you to understand, though," He said, "is that when I make you a promise, I've already written it in your book. It's as good as done. You just haven't made it to that chapter yet."

LEANING INTO GOD'S PROMISES FOR OUR LIVES IS LESS ABOUT WHAT WE HAVE TO DO TO MAKE IT HAPPEN, AND MORE ABOUT RECOGNIZING WHO HE IS.

HOW GOD MAKES PROMISES

Before you can know *what* God has promised you, you have to know *how* He's going to tell you about these things. In my own life, I have had promises from God show up in a number of ways. They can appear in dreams or visions, or by Him speaking to you. Sometimes He will even point you to a promise in the Bible that He wants you to focus on and apply to your own life. Remember that no promise He makes will ever contradict scripture. Just like you learned to hear His voice, you'll learn to discern His promises, too.

I'll give you an example of a promise He gave me back in 2020. My dad had been diagnosed with a very aggressive form of stomach cancer. Let's just say it didn't look good. The doctors wanted to start with an equally aggressive regimen of chemo and radiation. Once that shrunk the tumor slightly, they wanted to remove his stomach and part of his esophagus in order to decrease the likelihood of this type of cancer returning. All I could do was pray for him. Pray, pray, and pray some more. About a month or two into the whole thing, I had a dream. This was the first time in my life I had ever had a lucid dream. If you don't know what a lucid dream is, it's a dream where you're aware that you're dreaming. The best way I can describe it is that your body is asleep but your spirit is awake.

In this dream, I was sitting at my kitchen counter, journaling. I took a moment to look down at my hands and look around, observing the fact that I was fully coherent in my dream world. *How bizarre,* I thought. Out of the corner of my eye, I see a purple mist swirling around in my dining room as a cloud started to form. I got up from my seat and walked over to it to see what it was. As I approached, two hands reached out of the cloud, wanting to hold mine. It was at that point that I knew this was God. I took His hands. "Ask me what you want of me, my child," He spoke. With tears starting to form in my eyes, I pleaded, "I want you to heal my dad." "It is done," was His answer. Then the dream was over as quickly as it started.

The next six months were incredibly brutal. After my dad had his stomach removed, there were multiple complications with his surgery sites struggling to heal. He was in and out of the hospital and had multiple episodes where he would collapse out of the blue. There was even a full month where he couldn't have any food or drink by mouth. In order to keep his mouth from drying out, he would have to rinse with water and spit it back into a cup like you would at the dentist. The whole family was terrified. I wanted to be terrified, but I wouldn't let myself. Apart from my feet and artistic abilities, my selective stubbornness is also something I inherited from my father. I knew that I had to hold onto the promise God gave me. I knew that God Himself would not appear to me in a dream to deliver me a message He didn't mean.

Once we thought dad was out of the woods, the cancer came back on his liver. I wanted so badly to freak out. I wanted to yell and be angry and let the dam of my feelings give way and rush over everything. Instead, I held onto that promise for dear life. Next thing we know, we were being told that although the mass was still on my dad's liver, every single solitary sign of cancer cells miraculously vanished. My sister-in-law and I sat there crying in the middle of a Mexican restaurant when my mom called to give us the news. *It's true,* I thought, *everything God claims to be is true.* I finally had concrete evidence that God is exactly who He says He is. That was the moment when I knew that His promises would always be kept and that I could put my weight on the words He says and they would not give way. It sparked a hunger in me to learn everything that I could about Him. I wanted to get to know Him on a deeper level and find out everything else that He claimed to be. Long story short: when God promises you something, He means it, no matter what the circumstances may look like.

FINDING YOUR PROMISE

Seeking out God's promises for your life is kind of like asking Him to let you peek at the road map. He's not going to show you the whole thing, because then you would be tempted to do it on your own and not have to depend on or include Him. But the glimpses He gives show you a general direction to walk in. They almost serve as a compass for you along your journey. When you start to feel lost, you look at your promise to know that you are headed in the right direction.

So, how do you find your own promise for your specific journey? That's simple. You ask Him. If you need to, use the exercise I gave you on day one in order to document your conversation with Him. This is another one of those times where we're going to ask a question and wait expectantly for an answer. Ask Him if there are any specific areas He wants you to focus on and what His promises are for those things. Write them all down so that you don't forget them later on.

Whatever promise God gives you is probably not going to make much sense. In fact, it probably seems pretty darn impossible.

> GOD DOESN'T PROMISE YOU THINGS THAT YOU'RE CAPABLE
> OF FULFILLING ON YOUR OWN.

He promises things that can only be done with His help. This is how He proves Himself to His children over and over again. Don't let this scare you. Remember, the promise isn't for *you* to fulfill. And it's not for you to figure out. This is just a tool that God uses to teach you how to depend on Him for each and every step that needs to be taken. It's all a way to bring you under His wing, into a closer relationship with Him. That should be more comforting than scary.

Once you have your promise, it's time to back it up with scripture. Did you know that there are 8,810 promises in the Bible? That's a pretty large number. If the promise you just heard is really from God, it will align with one of those biblical promises, all you have to do is find which one. Now, I do want to point out that if God has made a specific promise to your current situation, you probably won't find that in the Bible verbatim. For example, if God has promised to provide for you if you quit your job in order to start full time ministry or move across the country and have no income to depend on, you could look to Phillipians 4:19, "And my God will meet all your needs according to the riches of his glory in Christ Jesus."

No matter what verse you find that applies to your current circumstances, you are able to apply it to your life and your situation right now. When God made the promise to Abraham to be the God of his descendants, that includes us. Which means that those promises made long ago can apply to our lives right now as well. This is the living Word of God, after all. It is not some history book written long ago that is only to tell us about the life and lineage of Jesus. It is meant to be the sword with which we fight our battles. How do you fight when the enemy is telling you that you are worthless and your life will never amount to anything? You find a biblical promise and cling to it for dear life.

This is a crucial part of contending for the promises for your life. You have to hang onto it. You'd better believe that the enemy will do everything in His power to keep you from hanging on, because the only way that that promise doesn't come true is if you let it go. Remember when the Israelites were rescued from slavery? They were on a journey into the Promised Land. But because they didn't believe in the promise even though God showed up for them time and time again, they didn't get to go. Instead, it was passed down to their children. Let's not let that happen to us.

That's exactly why it's important to make sure that the words you speak align with the promises God has given you. When the twelve Israelite spies were sent into the promised land to see what it was like, they already had the promise of God in their pocket. They knew that God had promised to give them this land. And yet, ten of them chose to misalign their words with that promise. They said that there was no way that it could be done because the circumstances didn't look ideal. Because the people who lived in that land were big and scary, they thought it must not be God's will. Because they would have to put in some work, they assumed the promise wasn't true. Allow me to point out that sometimes God will ask you to work towards your promise. It won't always be handed to you on a silver platter. But no matter what the promise looks like, you have to be certain that your words are not blocking that promise from coming to fruition. Joshua and Caleb were the only ones who got to go into the promised land because they were the only ones that believed what God said was true and came into agreement with it. If we want to see these promises come to pass, we have to continue to cling to them no matter what giants we face.

Now, I do want you to be on your guard, because the devil is sneaky. He will try to convince you that you're crazy, that you have no evidence for this promise, that it's been five years and nothing has happened so it must not be true, that you're denying reality by clinging to some fairytale. Believe me, I have heard all of those lies. And in the moments where I wasn't armoring myself with the Word of God, I almost believed them. Don't make the same mistakes that I made. Don't make the same mistakes that the Israelites made. Once you find that verse, read it every morning. Every single time one of those lies from the enemy comes to your mind, recite that verse out loud. Memorize it. Speak it often.

Remember how Psalm 119:105 says, "Your word is a lamp for my feet and a light on my path."? If you don't use the Word of God to light your pathway to the promised land, you will be stumbling the whole way, I can promise you that. Use your Bible like the weapon that it was intended to be and do not give the enemy a single inch of your God-given territory.

WAITING FOR THE PROMISE

I remember going to meet with a mentor of mine shortly after I received one of my first promises from God. I felt crazy. And when I say crazy, I mean Noah building an ark in the desert before he even knew what rain was crazy. This promise was massive and impossible. It was a God-sized dream, that was for sure. Hesitantly, I told this woman what I believed God had told me. I waited patiently for her to get out her phone and dial my family's numbers to schedule an intervention. Instead, she didn't flinch. She didn't even blink. Her response was,

"Yep. That sounds like God to me." She said it as casually as if she were reciting what she ate for breakfast.

After I recovered from the shock of someone actually believing my wild story, I continued, "The thing is, I haven't told anyone about this for months. When God asked me if I would do this, I told Him, 'Yes,' but nothing has happened yet." Oh, sweet, naive little Caitlin. She thought that her God-sized dreams would come true at the snap of a finger. How precious. I'm sure my mentor was having to stifle her laughter as she replied, "Well, of course not. There's always a waiting period. That's the most important part." At the time, I had no idea what she meant by that, but three years into waiting for the promise to come to pass, I was starting to get the idea.

Waiting for the promise is an absolutely vital part of this journey. This is where life is breathed into them. Think of it kind of like pregnancy. You don't get to hold the baby just a few short days after that test turns positive. First, you have to let the baby develop. You have to let it grow to its full potential until you are ready and able to handle caring for it. It is important to note, however, that not all waiting periods are going to look the same. If you and someone else were promised the exact same thing at the exact same time, chances are, the journey to get there will look different for each of you. That's because we serve a deeply personal God. He's not interested in following formulas, He's interested in you. So He's going to carry out your promise according to what timing is important for your specific journey.

> TRY NOT TO COMPARE THE GESTATION OF YOUR DREAMS TO ANYONE ELSE'S.

Did you know that a possum gives birth within about two weeks of becoming pregnant? However, an elephant takes 22 months to grow their babies. Sometimes the bigger the promise is, the longer it takes to come to pass. But I promise you, this is a process that you do not want to rush.

Think about it like baking. Sometimes when my kids don't eat all of the bananas I've bought, I will make banana bread. I've never really been a massive fan of banana bread, but I figured it's better than letting the bananas go to waste. Until one day, I found the most incredible recipe for banana bread that I have ever tasted. The only downside was the amount of time that went into preparing it. Instead of putting the bananas straight into the batter, you first slow roast the bananas for 15 minutes. Instead of adding the butter right away, you brown it first. But when I tell you that my family ate that entire loaf of banana bread in one day, I'm not joking. God isn't trying to hand you a half-baked dream. He loves you enough to take the time to slow roast every ingredient. But trust me when I say that all of that preparation is going to be well worth it when it comes out of the oven.

Now, rather than twiddling your thumbs and waiting for God to do the work, there are some things that you can do to help the process along. In fact, I would even go so far as to say that your effort, to some extent, is necessary. Remember when we were talking about the story of the Israelites in the wilderness? They had been enslaved in Egypt for over 400 years before that. Slavery was the only form of society that they had ever known. When they got to the wilderness, God gave them The 10 commandments, as well as a whole laundry list of laws and regulations that they are now supposed to live by. Why? Do you think it was because God didn't want them to have any fun? Was it because He's a harsh taskmaster who can never be pleased? No. It's because although He had just taken them out of Egypt, Egypt now had to be taken out of them. They had developed some deeply ingrained habits from living in Egypt that God didn't want them carrying with them into the promised land. If they had cooperated and embraced this new way of living, they would have made it to the promised land in a much shorter amount of time. Instead, they complained and called God cruel. He gave them chance after chance to right their wrongs and get with the program until finally, it became clear that they never would. Because of their actions, or, arguably, lack thereof, He had to make it so that they would have to pass the promise on to the next generation. How sad. Don't let that happen to you, my friend.

What about Abraham and Sarah? God had promised them a son, and, in addition to that, an entire nation of people that would come from that son. Yet rather than believing God and waiting for their promise to come to fruition, they tried to take matters into their own hands. Abraham did have a son, but not through his beloved wife first. Instead, Hagar (Sarah's maidservant) gave birth to Ishmael and some reality-TV level drama ensued. Not only did Ishmael's existence create tension between Sarah and Hagar, but once Isaac (the promised son) was born, Ishmael persecuted him. The takeaway from this story? Don't take the banana bread out of the oven early. Don't rush the promise. You don't want to create an Ishmael in your life by trying to make your promises come to pass in your own strength.

How about Joseph? If you've ever studied that story, you'll see that Joseph really did most everything by the book. The only reason his brothers hated him was because he was daddy's favorite. Okay, maybe he was a little arrogant when he told his brothers about the dream that God gave him, revealing that they would bow down to him one day. But other than that, he seemed to be morally upstanding for the rest of his life. He was sold into slavery, but he did such a great job that he was put in charge of Potipher's house. Then when Potipher's wife tried to make a pass at him, he politely told her, "no way" and avoided her at all costs. But that honesty caused Potiphar's wife to be angry and have him thrown in prison. Once he was in prison, he was so responsible that they put him in charge there, too. He continued to use his God-given gifts to interpret dreams for people, politely asking them to return the favor and yet he was still stuck in prison for another two years before his promise finally came to pass. Can you see any major blunders in his story? Me neither.

Here's the thing about Joseph's story: it was all about the timing. Joseph didn't do anything wrong to delay his promise. He cooperated and even excelled at every task he was given the entire way. But it was the dream of the famine that brought him into Pharaoh's courts and caused him to be elevated. In the meantime, God was laying all of the dominoes out so that they would fall at just the right time. He was working in the hearts of Joseph's family, letting little Benjamin grow old enough to make the journey to Egypt with his older brothers, teaching Joseph about stewardship and responsibility even in the face of adversity. It was all necessary in order to tie the story together with a neat little bow.

> SOMETIMES, THE REASON WHY OUR PROMISES TAKE SO LONG IS BECAUSE THEY HAVE TO HAPPEN IN GOD'S PERFECT TIMING, NOT OURS.

What about when the promise doesn't come true? You can wait and wait all you want, but sometimes things don't always pan out the way that you want them to, do they? I recently heard a different perspective on the story of Moses.[1] In Exodus, we read about God promising to take Moses and the Israelites through the wilderness and into the

Promised Land. He's even so specific that He tells Moses exactly where the borders will be and exactly what they should do when they get there. The thing is, there was a situation where God instructed Moses to speak to a rock so that water would come forth out of it for the people. Instead of speaking to the rock, Moses gets angry and hits it with his staff. The people still got their water, but because of Moses' disobedience to God, he is informed that he will not be allowed to enter the promised land and will instead see it from a distance before dying in the wilderness. How sad, right? You might read that story and think that God went back on His original promise. Remember how I told you there would be times where you doubt God's goodness? Case in point. And yet, if we skip ahead to the New Testament, we see a story of Jesus taking Peter, James and John up into the mountains where He transforms into His glorious form, a bright white light, before their very eyes. And who appears with Him on the Mount of Transfiguration? Elijah and Moses. Do you want to take a wild guess as to where the Mount of Transfiguration is located? That's right, it's in the Promised Land.

You see, even after the physical death of Moses, God kept His promise. If that doesn't speak to the limitlessness of our God, I don't know what does. We tend to think of the death of our physical bodies as the end of something. As if God only has a short window of time to work in our lives. But the departure of our physical bodies is the beginning of eternity. We view it as the end, whereas God views that as just the beginning. Hebrews 11:13 says, "All these people were still living by faith when they died. They did not receive the things promised; they only saw them from a distance, admitting that they were foreigners and strangers on earth." When I read that verse, I see great examples of faith, yes, but I also see that this life is not where we end. Those people recognized that they were foreigners and strangers on earth, meaning that they realized that this world was not their home. They understood that we serve a really big God who is capable of fulfilling His promises even after we have parted ways with our physical bodies. We see in James 4:14 that our lives on this earth are a mist that appears for a little while and then vanishes. And yet if God is still capable of doing so much in our physical lifetimes, just imagine what He could do with all of eternity.

To really put this into perspective, I want you to imagine what the word eternity means. It's only fitting to talk about eternity in a book that's all about limitlessness, right? I once heard it described like this: If you were to take all of the sand from all over the world and pile it in one large pile, imagine how big that pile would be. I'm not just talking about beaches here, I mean every beach, the bottom of every ocean, every sand trap on a golf course, and every sand box on every playground in all the world. That would be a pretty big pile, wouldn't it? Now imagine that a bird comes every 100,000 years and takes a single grain of sand from that pile and moves it to the opposite side of the earth. Once the entire pile of sand is moved, the bird moves it back and forth over and over and over again. That is just a glimpse of how long eternity is. And yet, we somehow have adopted the idea that God is going to do everything He plans to do within the small window of time that this earth is in existence. I would encourage you not to limit God to your lifetime. There will be many more exciting things that are still to take place in the eternity that's to come. All it takes is that simple mindset shift for you to stop living in the bondage of anxiety and unlock the faith you have in your Creator.

STEWARDING THE PROMISE

When looking at these biblical examples, there's lots of takeaways we can learn from. Of course, you are always free to make your own mistakes, I just find that it's much faster and much less painful to learn from the stories of others. The important thing to remember is that there is still work to be done while you wait for these promises to come to pass. Maybe God has promised you financial prosperity. There's a good chance that He will want you to learn about stewarding your finances well while you wait. Get a budgeting app, start tithing, stop buying iced coffee every day, and begin to manage your money well. Maybe you're desperately wanting to have a baby. He may ask you to deal with the heart wounds from your own childhood first so that you don't pass that pain along to future generations. Maybe He's promised you a spouse, but He wants you to learn how to be loved by Him first so that you don't enter into a codependent relationship that would cause you more heartache than fulfillment. Believe me, friend, the waiting is for your benefit.

I had a hard time grasping that concept. In fact, I remember telling God that it felt cruel for God to tell me about the promise that far ahead of time. It was almost like He was dangling a carrot in front of my face that I was chasing but couldn't reach. But in His goodness, He so graciously explained to me what was really going on. This was what He said:

> "Imagine you're a kid and your parents ask you if you
> want to get a puppy. You reply, 'Of course, I want
> a puppy!' And they're response is, 'Well, then let's
> work on becoming a little more responsible and we
> will get you a puppy. Let's start with learning to clean

your room.' As a child, you wouldn't want to do the mundane tasks to make you more responsible, but without the promise of a puppy, you wouldn't have the motivation to accomplish those mundane things that need to be worked on."

You see, rather than God telling us what to do without telling us why, He gives us something to look forward to at the end of it. That's how much of a loving Father He is. He doesn't have to reward you at all, and yet, He delights in it because of His love for you. Pretty neat, huh?

So rather than focusing on how long you'll have to wait or how many boring things you'll have to do before your promise gets here, focus instead on the goodness of God. Do not forfeit your promise by complaining like the Israelites. Don't try to take matters into your own hands like Abraham and Sarah, and trust in God's timing like Joseph.

> BECAUSE WHEN YOU DELIGHT YOURSELF IN HIM, HE MAKES
> EVERY STEP OF THE JOURNEY AN ADVENTURE.

THE DIFFERENCE BETWEEN PROMISE AND DESIRE

I believe that sometimes the reason why we struggle to believe that God will fulfill His promises is because we haven't quite yet seen Him fulfill our desires. Of course, the Bible does say that God will give you the desires of our hearts and that we are to ask Him for those things,[2] but we forget that sometimes He has to walk us through the process of refinement before He will fulfill those desires. And as we walk through that refinement, many times, those desires will change.

For most of my life, I have struggled with friendships. I was always a shy kid with a healthy dose of social awkwardness. Maybe it was God's way of ingraining humility in me from the get go, I'm not sure. I used to watch shows like *Friends* and *How I Met Your Mother* and envy the tight knit groups that those fictional characters had. I craved that level of loyalty and community. They always had someone to go to lunch with, always had someone to talk to about their problems, and always had someone to jump in and help whenever they needed it. I decided that that was something my life was missing, and I begged God for it for years. I would have a few friendships sprinkled throughout my life, and at one point, I even had a group of friends that I could call myself a part of, but it was never quite like I pictured it. It didn't bring that sense of fulfillment and camaraderie that I was longing for.

As God began to walk me through the process of refinement and led me into a deeper relationship with Him, I started to learn that my desire was all wrong. I had been looking for loyalty and acceptance from an outside source, yet God was right in front of me all along. He became my friend. He showed me the loyalty and acceptance and unwavering friendship that I had been hungry for all along. I didn't need a whole group of imperfect people to fill that void, I had a whole trinity of perfection right in front of my face the entire time. And so, my desires began to shift. I no longer felt the need to have those close-knit friendships in order to bring a sense of community to my life. Jesus became the one I spent my time with, God was the one I took my problems to, and the Holy Spirit began to help me through the trickiest of situations. Sometimes our desires are just our way of trying to shove something else into a God-sized hole in our hearts. If your desires align with God's will for you, of course He wants to give them to you. But if your desires are feeble attempts to replace Him, those wishes may not come true. Trust me, the times when He withholds your desires from you are often for your benefit. Most of the time, desires are something that we concoct in our own heart that line up with our own vision for our lives. God's promises are the type of things that we could never cook up on our own, and they're often far better than anything we could want for ourselves.

My son loves monster trucks. There was one year when he asked for a few specific trucks for his birthday. Little did he know, his daddy had bought tickets for us to go to Monster Jam and see some real monster trucks just a few weeks later. The monster truck was his desire, and the tickets to Monster Jam were a promise. Because his desire aligned with his father's promise, he got the monster trucks he wanted and even took them into the stadium with him as he watched the real monster trucks race around the dirt track. When our desires line up with God's plan for our life, why wouldn't He give them to us? He's a good father, after all. It's only when our desires conflict with His plan that He might say no and give us something better instead.

WHAT IF YOU DON'T HAVE A PROMISE?

Listen, I don't want it to sound like a promise is vital to your relationship with God and that you cannot move forward without one. You absolutely can. Sometimes, God waits to reveal our promises to us until we're ready. If He's not giving you a promise just yet, don't sweat it. He may want you to focus on other things first like learning how to hear His voice, learning about who He is, and figuring out who you are (we'll talk more about identity tomorrow).

You may be wondering how you're supposed to move forward without having a promise for your life. What are you supposed to do?

What steps should you take? Let me encourage you that you *do* have a promise for your life, it just may not be revealed yet.

> GOD ALREADY KNOWS THE PLAN, AND BECAUSE HE IS OM-
> NISCIENT, THAT MEANS HE ALSO KNOWS THE EXACT RIGHT
> TIME TO REVEAL IT TO YOU.

In the meantime, try not to put too much pressure on figuring things out. God can use quite literally anything you do in this season for your benefit.

When I was pregnant with my son, I decided that I wanted to design his nursery and renovate it myself (with a little help from family). Once it was all finished, seeing the whole room come together was such a rush of dopamine. I loved watching each piece I hand selected weave together to tell a story in a way that communicated all of the hopes and dreams that I had for my baby boy. Because I enjoyed it so much, I started delving into a lot more DIY projects and renovating our entire house one chunk at a time. There was no divine purpose behind my decision, I was just doing something that seemed like fun. Not to mention, I was really tired of looking at the brown carpet. Several years later, God revealed one of my promises to me, which involved designing and renovating a large property. I had no idea that my fun little projects were really preparing me for a larger promise, but that just goes to show how resourceful God is. He wastes nothing.

> ANYTHING YOU OCCUPY YOUR TIME WITH IN THE WAITING,
> HE CAN USE IT AS AN INVESTMENT IN YOUR PROMISE.

One thing that I really want you to become familiar with is how to be content as you wait on the promises of God, trusting that He will reveal everything that needs to be revealed at the exact right time. If you have no clue what the promises for your life entail, I would highly encourage you to have fun in the meantime. God once explained it to me like a child waiting for their dinner. I was so fixated on figuring out what to do with my life that I was checking in with Him every five minutes, like a child asking when their dinner would be ready. He told me, "Just go play. I will tell you when it's time to eat." Although it is our job to seek Him, it's not our job to decide on timing. We don't have to ask when our dinner will be ready. We can rest assured that when the time is right, He will meet us exactly where we are and give us the next steps.

I do want to remind you that if you have accepted Jesus as Lord of your life, you are already living out one of the biggest promises that anyone can have spoken over their life. You are living out your salvation. While it's good to seek everything that God has for our lives, it's important that we first recognize that simply being His child is enough. Even if He never gives you a revelation, never teaches you anything, or never performs a miracle on your behalf, the God of the universe still chose to adopt you into His family. Your status as His child is more than enough to fill your life with purpose.

3

IDENTITY

Do you know who you are? I mean, do you really know? We're all on some sort of journey to discover our true identity, right? Before we're even able to speak, we have some level of ability to express our likes and dislikes, but as life unfolds, it's the situations around us that seem to mold who we become. If you had a bad relationship with your parents, you may find it difficult to trust or be vulnerable with other people. You may have even branded that as "part of your personality," but do you really believe that that's true? Or is it possible that those deep wounds shaped your identity over time?

> LEARNING OUR IDENTITY IN CHRIST IS SIMPLY A PROCESS OF SHEDDING THE IDENTITY THAT WE (OR THE SITUATIONS AROUND US) HAVE MOLDED US INTO AND GETTING BACK TO WHO WE WERE ORIGINALLY CREATED TO BE.

As God once told me, "We're not working towards the best version of yourself, we're working towards who you've always been."

Finding God's promises for our lives is often the first step to discovering our identity. Abraham didn't live in the identity of a father until God promised him that he would be the father of nations. Joseph was the youngest brother, which typically meant last-in-line in his household. He didn't step into the identity of a ruler until God gave him the dream that he would rule over his brothers. Our promises point to our God-given identity, but first, we have to undergo the arduous process of stripping away the identities that we've adopted for ourselves.

When I was younger, my grandparents used to live right across the street. Sometimes, my grandfather would call me to help him pick the vegetables from the garden or shell peas or crack pecans for fresh-baked pecan pie. My hands would ache from hours of squeezing those metal nut crackers until I heard the satisfying snap of the pecan shell. But that was only half of the battle. Once the shell was open, you had to dig out the pecan, inspect it for signs of rot, and scrape the dirt out of the crevices with what looked like a dental pick. Let me tell you, those pecans seemed awfully fond of their shells. They did not want to let them go. However, if you were unsuccessful at fully removing the shell and all of the dirt, you would wind up with a horribly bitter batch of pecans and all of your hard work would be for nothing.

Just like those pecans, getting to your true identity is a process. First, you have to allow yourself to be cracked open and pried loose from that old identity that you have clung to for so long. Next, you have to invite Him to remove any rotten pieces where those deep heart wounds have prevented you from being whole. Then, you have to undergo tedious amounts of refining and removing that old dirt that has seeped its way deep into your innermost being. It takes quite a bit of time, but the end result is so savory.

IDENTITY AS HIS CHILD

A question I get quite often is "How do I even know if I am saved? I mean, I think I am. I just don't know how to be certain." The first step in learning your identity is acknowledging your identity. You can't foster a relationship with God if you're uncertain if you're even a part of His family yet. While we are all made in God's image, that doesn't automatically make us a part of His family. Just like simply believing that God exists doesn't make you a part of His family either. We have to decide that we want Him to adopt us. We have to tell Him that we want to be His child. The good news is, His answer to that is always yes! Becoming a part of His family can feel a little strange at first. You might not feel any different, and it might take some time to get to know Him and see the growth in your life, but that doesn't mean the change hasn't happened. If you've committed yourself to Him, you're a part of the family, even if you don't see the changes right away.

Let's say that you decide one day that you want to become a runner. What do you do? You get out there and run, right? That first day, you may not even be able to run to your mailbox without getting winded, but does that make you any less of a runner? What matters is your commitment. If you're dedicated to running everyday, then the distance doesn't matter. The amount of time you've been training is arbitrary. You are just as much of a runner on day one as you are on day 453 because your commitment is the same.

Now, on the other hand, just because you call yourself a runner doesn't mean that you are one. You could have all the equipment, have done all the research, and know all of the statistics. But if you're not lacing up your shoes and putting your feet to the pavement, you're not a runner, my friend. You can be a biblical theologian, but if you don't have a personal relationship with God, all of that knowledge goes to waste. You have to invite Him into your heart and your life. If you're willing to do that, He will work out the rest. Evaluate your level of commitment, that's all it takes.

Once you've identified yourself as being a child of God, we need to talk about what that looks like. In order to know how being His child impacts your life, we first need to discuss the kind of father He is. I understand that for most people, imperfect relationships with your earthly parents can unfairly taint your view on your relationship with God. There are things that need to be learned and things that need to be unlearned (removing the pecan shell, remember?).

First, let's talk about what the love of God looks like. For many of us, love takes on a bunch of different meanings. Some might equate sex with love, for others, it could look like codependency. Just because those are our unique definitions of love, doesn't make those definitions true. We need to understand what love looks like in order to understand what it doesn't look like. The simplest way I can explain this is by pointing you to 1 Corinthians 13: 4-8. Let's read through it together.

"Love is patient. Love is kind. It does not envy, it does not boast, it is not proud. It does not dishonor others, it is not self-seeking, it is not easily angered, it keeps no record of wrongs. Love does not delight in evil, but rejoices with the truth. It always protects, always trusts, always hopes, always perseveres. Love never fails."

You see, God is love in its purest, truest form. Therefore, God's love encompasses all of the attributes listed above. So in order to know if some of your thoughts about God's love are correct or not, compare them to this scripture. Do you think that God is angry at you for making mistakes? Well, that scripture tells us that love keeps no record of wrongs so that can't be true. Do you think that God is fine with you continuing to live in sin because He "knows your heart"? Well, that scripture says that love does not delight in evil, so that myth is debunked. Maybe you even think that God is mad at you or ashamed of you for not coming to Him sooner. "Love is patient, love is kind." Do you see where I'm going with this?

If we jump over to 2 Corinthians 10:5, we see that it says to "take every thought captive and make it obedient to Christ." That means that whenever you have a thought that enters your mind, you examine it for any evidence of scriptural truth. If it's devoid of that truth, you toss it out of the window. I want to encourage you to begin to examine the thoughts you have about God and see if they are true or not. Romans 12:2 commands us to "be transformed by the renewing of your mind." This is where the change happens. The shift starts to take place when you begin to adjust your mindset. I'd like to reiterate that YOU are the one who has to change your mindset. God is a gentleman, not an enforcer. He will not work in your life without your permission. Just because you've accepted Him as your Savior does not mean your life will automatically make a 180 degree turn. You have to continue to be dedicated to your training, just like running.

Now, just like any good parent, God will also correct His children. I know this seems daunting to some people because they have a tendency to picture God as this angry being sitting on His throne with a lightning bolt in hand, ready to smite them at the first given opportunity. Nothing could be further from the truth. His corrections are so very gentle. Love is patient, love is kind, right?

Remember when I told you that my husband and I recently adopted some equines and we had to go over the rules of interacting with those animals with my kids? One day, after we had had the animals for a few weeks, my son forgot the rule about walking behind our donkey. Rather than panicking, I gently said, "Hey bud, come over here to me. Remember, we don't want to walk behind the donkey in case he kicks. I don't want you to get injured." My son's response was immediate compliance. I called him to come closer to me so that he would be protected. Marinate on that for a second.

Sometimes all we have to do when we mess up is come closer to God so that He can protect us from the harm that those guidelines were meant to prevent us from in the first place. By the way that I explained these guidelines, my son understood that they were for his protection, so he was happily obedient. He didn't want to get kicked in the head, and he knew that that instruction was to prevent his injury. Whenever God corrects us, He always does so in a way that helps us understand that it is for our benefit. When we learned what God's voice sounds like, we talked about how it never brings shame or condemnation. The same is true for His corrections.

Another thing that I want you to remember is that discipline always serves a purpose. Think about some of the reasons why you would reprimand a child. Throwing tantrums is the first thing that comes to my mind, and it seems to be something all tiny humans have in common. Why would I discipline my children when they throw a tantrum? Because I want to teach them how to be in control of their emotions rather than allowing their emotions to control them. I want to teach them how to become self-disciplined. Self-control is a fruit of the Spirit, remember? Discipline begets discipline.

> SOMETIMES WE HAVE TO BE DISCIPLINED SO THAT WE CAN
> LEARN HOW TO BE SELF-DISCIPLINED.

Now that you have some sort of idea what He looks like as your Father, let's discuss what your behavior should look like as His child. The easiest way for me to digest this concept is to look at my own children. I have learned more about what my relationship with God looks like through my children than through anything else. A relationship with God requires that same level of connection. It's really difficult to get close to someone you never spend time with. Now, spending time with them doesn't always have to look like work. Newborn babies can't do any of that and yet they still form close bonds with their parents through close, intimate contact. And so if you're just starting your relationship with God or you're just now taking it seriously, it might be a good idea to just sit in His presence and let Him hold you for a while.

HEALTHY RELATIONSHIP

Most of us have a tendency to gravitate towards one person in the trinity, identifying them as our unspoken favorite. A lot of people have a tendency to view Jesus as their friend, God as a judgemental ruler, and the Holy Spirit as an optional addition for the charismatic folks. At least, that was kind of how I understood it at first. The thing is, while each one in the trinity serves a different role, they are all comprised of the same characteristics with the same personality. They are unchanging. In fact, I think the Trinity gives us the best example of what a family is supposed to look like. You have a loving authority figure, a close friend, and a nurturer. What more could you want out of a family?

One thing that I did for far too long was ignore 2/3rds of the Trinity. I spoke to Jesus and Jesus only for a large portion of my life. When my dad was diagnosed with cancer, that was when I took the time to acknowledge the Holy Spirit, who then led me to the Father to show me who I was. Since the relationship with the Heavenly Father seems to be the most complicated relationship for people to accept at times, I want to break it down for you as best I can.

In order to understand this relationship a little better, let's take a look at an example that I think we all know and love: Simba and Mufasa. If you haven't seen *The Lion King* yet, first of all, where have you been? Second, you might want to go check it out before I ruin the whole movie for you in the next few paragraphs. Simba was a far-from-perfect child while Mufasa was a nearly perfect parent. That doesn't make the gravity of their love any less beautiful. Let's explore how this story can help us to better understand what a healthy relationship with our Father should look like.

We can all agree that a healthy, loving relationship between a parent and a child means that they have to spend time together, right? The movie opens with a scene where Simba is trying to wake his father up so that they can spend the day together. Simba is desperate to learn from Mufasa, desperate to be in his presence. He's not concerned with whether or not He's inconveniencing his father, and he's not wondering if his father has better things to do. He approaches Mufasa like a true child: ready and willing to spend the day together. When we approach God in the same way, it puts us in a heart posture that is ready to receive. If you're too busy worrying about whether or not God actually wants to spend time with you, you're not acting like His child, and your mind isn't ready to learn whatever He might want to teach you. Let's start by approaching each day with excitement, aching to see whatever it is that God wants to show us. I promise you, God is not inconvenienced or annoyed. Unlike Mufasa, you don't have to wake Him up. He's been up, just waiting for you to join Him for the day.

In addition to being more than willing to spend time with us, God is always at the ready to defend His children whenever necessary. Do you remember that interaction between Mufasa and Scar where Scar is trying to diminish the importance of Simba by insulting him right to his father's face? What was Mufasa's reaction? He demanded that his child be respected as an heir to the throne. Psalm 105:15 says, "Do not touch my anointed ones; do my prophets no harm." That could be followed up with Romans 12:19 (NKJV), "Beloved, do not avenge yourselves, but rather give place to wrath; for it is written, 'Vengeance is mine, I will repay,' says the Lord." God makes it pretty clear where He stands when it comes to His kids. *Do not touch them.* Sometimes, it's difficult for us to see God as our defender because He often defends us behind our backs. Simba wasn't around to see this interaction between Mufasa and Scar take place, but his dad had his back, nonetheless.

Don't think that His loyalty has anything to do with your actions, though. Time and time again God has rescued us even in the midst of our disobedience. Just like when Simba went to the shadowlands after his father warned him not to. He gets captured by hyenas, and Mufasa comes to his aid and scares the hyenas half to death in the process. Do you remember the story of the prodigal son? That son knew he had done wrong, and although he was filled with shame and guilt because of his actions, he decided to go back to his father's house. You can read all about it in Luke 15. Verse 20 says, "But while he was still a long way off, his father saw him and was filled with compassion for him;

he ran to his son, threw his arms around him and kissed him." God is not holding your mistakes over your head. His love is patient and kind, keeping no record of wrongs, remember? Whenever you mess up, simply acknowledging it and asking God for help causes Him to run to you. He loves coming to our rescue, and we can expect that He's bringing the same amount of extravagant love and compassion shown to the prodigal son with Him.

Now, just because He rescues us whenever we mess up doesn't mean He wants us to keep falling into that trap. In the part of the movie where Simba deliberately disobeys Mufasa, Mufasa still has to correct his son so that nothing like that ever happens again. After he explains to his son that his choices were dangerous for himself and others, he then proceeds to get on Simba's level, connect with him, and use it as a bonding opportunity. He wraps it up by reminding Simba that he will always be there to guide him. We can expect the same from God.

> HIS CORRECTION ALWAYS LEADS TO A DEEPER CONNECTION.

He's not angry with you for making a mistake, but He does want you to learn from it.

Another thing we can expect from our Father is that He will always protect us, even at His own expense. We all remember the scene where Simba gets caught in a stampede and Mufasa rushes to his aid, throwing caution to the wind as he sets out to protect his son. Ultimately, that choice led to his own demise. I'm sure you're aware of the fact that Jesus sacrificed Himself for you, but do you realize that He chose to do that from the beginning? Think about it. If God is all-knowing, and able to see past, present, and future, that means that He knew exactly what was going to happen when He created humans with free will. He knew that Satan was going to rebel and be kicked out of heaven. He knew that Satan would then tempt Adam and Eve in the garden and they would fall for it. He also knew that that mistake would cause Him to have to come down here and save us Himself. And yet, He chose to give us free will anyway. Let that sink in for a second. He knew every mistake you would ever make in your entire life, and He gave you the freedom to choose that anyway, because He knew that He was willing to sacrifice Himself for you. If you ever doubt the Father's love for you, go back and read that last paragraph again. Love always protects.

Unfortunately, as Simba's story continues to unfold, we see that his guilt and shame causes him to run from his identity and his calling. When we catch up with him as an adult, it seems as though he has lost himself and lost his way. He lives in complete denial of everything he has ever known in order to shroud himself in an identity that's less painful to face. Does that sound familiar? At some point or another, that's what all of us do. We adhere to something that's less painful than the truth and adopt it as our personality. We've all done it, but let's see what happens when he finally decides to face the past.

As he's searching for answers, he comes upon a pool of water where he sees his father's reflection in his own. Suddenly, his father appears to him in a vision and says, "You have forgotten who you are, and so, forgotten me." When we stray away from our God-given identity, we forget that we were made in His image in the first place. We were created to resemble our Father. It's only when we stray away from that that our identity begins to shift from its original design. Mufasa closes his speech by saying, "Remember who you are." We must do the same. By remembering who our Father is, we're reminded of how much we were designed to be like Him. Whenever you recognize that, you begin to step into it. Simba makes the bold decision to go back home and take back his rightful identity as king. This means that he must fight and defeat his enemy along the way, but in the end, he is victorious because he remembered his true identity.

IDENTITY AS HIS BRIDE

Do you know that the Bible often compares Christ followers to being the "Bride of Christ"? That may sound really confusing to some. I thought I was His child? Now I'm His bride? That makes no sense. Jesus often spoke in parables and analogies to help us understand things better. Remember the running analogy I gave you earlier? You're labeled as a runner because of your commitment, not because of your ability. Think of this the same way. It's just a metaphor.

Whenever my pastor[1] is asked the question, "How do I know if I'm saved or not?", he likes to respond by asking, "Well, how do you know if you're married or not? Do you have to think about it?" Our relationship with God is determined by our commitment to Him, just as one would commit themselves to another person in marriage, but our relationship to Him as His child is because we are made in His image and adopted into His family whenever we make that commitment. It's a metaphorical way of helping our human brains come to some sort of understanding of the ways of God. I hope that clears up some of the confusion.

Oftentimes, when you hear people talking about committing their life to Christ, it's followed up by the conversation of water baptism. One day, I asked God why baptism was so important to Him. I knew that we follow salvation with baptism because we saw Jesus set that example before He began His ministry, but I was struggling to fully grasp the significance of it. God's response to me was "Why do you wear a wedding ring?" I replied, "It's a symbol of my commitment to my husband. I want other people to see that I'm proud to be his wife." His response caused me to stop and think. "I want my bride to be proud that I'm her husband, too," He replied. If that doesn't make you tear up, check your pulse. We have to remember that although God is the all-powerful, all-knowing creator of the universe, He still has feelings. He doesn't need us, but He *wants* us. How incredible is that?

A few weeks ago, I was spending some time with God on my afternoon walk. All of a sudden, He gives me this vision. I was in a wedding dress with an extremely thick veil, the kind you couldn't see my face through. I was walking down the aisle and saw Jesus standing there waiting for me. As I stood in front of Him, He lifted my veil, revealing my face. With an incredible look of love in His eyes, He kissed my hand, turned me towards the crowd of people watching and began to show me off. That was the first time that it ever clicked in my mind that I am His bride. I had spent all of this time learning about who He was as my father and what a relationship as His daughter was supposed to be, but neglecting the fact that I was His bride. I started to do a deep dive into what that really meant.

You see, my identity as a wife and my identity as a daughter are two drastically different things. My parents had raised me to be a very independent person. I was the eldest daughter in my family. My brother was very actively involved in a lot of different activities, both of my parents had full-time careers, and my sister was five years younger than me. So my parents taught me pretty early on about the value of responsibility. Because of that, I learned how to handle the things that needed to get done.

When I met my husband, my father-in-law seemed very impressed by how independent I was. He's often told me, "I love how you don't wait around for other people to do things for you. You find a way to make it work." I wore that compliment like a badge of honor, because it was true. I didn't *need* other people. I was self-sufficient.

And yet, when I became a wife, my role drastically shifted. During the early years of our marriage, my husband was gone a good bit for work. Whenever he was gone, I would shift back into my old role of independence and hold down the fort. It made me a good partner to my husband because he knew that he didn't have to worry about anything while he was gone. And yet, when he would come home, I willingly took a step back because I understood that the husband's role is to lead his home. When Josh is home, I let him do some of the things that I know I am perfectly capable of doing myself because I understand that this marriage is not about what *I* do. It is about what we do together.

And yet, I had not been filling those shoes as the bride of Christ. I was still living in the daughter identity, where I needed to depend on myself and get things done in my own strength, and neglecting the task of letting God take care of me. My thinking was that I am a talented, resourceful person who is capable of taking care of myself when I need to, so why wouldn't I? The answer is because if I am depending on myself, then I'm not giving God the opportunity to show me that I don't have to do it on my own. The same can be said of many different areas of my life. Learning how to become His bride means that we have to have a healthy understanding of what marriage roles were designed to look like in the first place.

In order to understand marriage roles, let's go all the way back to the beginning. When God first created Adam, He said "It is not good for man to be alone. I will make a helper suitable for him." Genesis 2:18. Another translation says "one who will balance him." We can conclude from this passage that our role as a wife, first and foremost is to be a helpmate to our husbands. One who will balance them out and propel them forward.

What does being a helpmate actually look like? It means that we help our husband's vision for the family come to pass. I want to pause for a moment and point out that I am talking about a healthy marriage relationship here, the way it was designed. If, for example, you are in a marriage where your husband is an atheist and his vision for your family is for you all to stop going to church, obviously that is not in line with God's will for your life and your household. But if we are discussing what it looks like to follow a godly husband as he seeks God's will for his family, it only makes sense that we would not oppose him on that but would instead help that vision come to fruition. See, this is what it really means to be God's bride. It means that we are helping God's vision for this earth come to pass by supporting and carrying it out.

We can't carry out God's vision if we are compromising. Romans 12:2 says, "Do not conform to the patterns of this world, but be transformed by the renewing of your mind." In order to understand His will, we have to get to know Him by reading His word AND spending time in His presence. Do not miss this: you need BOTH.

Once we understand His vision, how are we supposed to carry it out? By using our God-given authority. Let me explain. I'm a stay-at-home mom because, at this point in time, that was the decision that made the most sense for our family. Most of the time, we are solely reliant on my husband's income. Now, let's say that my husband calls me and tells me that He wants to get his dad a really nice gift for his birthday. He's already decided what he wants to get him, all he needs me to do is go get it and deliver it. Because he and I have a joint bank account, I can go down to the bank and withdraw funds on my husband's behalf even if I have not contributed a single dime to that account. Why? Because I have access to it. And with that access, I can carry out the vision of blessing the person my husband wants to bless.

As God's wife, we have access to His account. We have access to all of the same power and authority that Jesus had. God didn't make a special separate bank account for Jesus. If we study and follow the teachings of Jesus, we can see that His entire ministry was teaching us how to make withdrawals from that account and carry out the Father's vision. All we need to do is continue to carry it out to the best of our ability.

IDENTITY AS AN INDIVIDUAL

In addition to being a child and a bride, you're also an individual with a unique purpose and a unique identity. This is the part where I see most people getting tripped up, because they have an understanding of the biblical principles of their identity, but they seem to think that it stops there, that they are just a drop in the ocean and have no individual purpose apart from the greater good. I get it, because I used to be there. I kind of thought of it like a company. God was the CEO and I was an employee. Of course, the CEO would care about me on some level because they cared about the company and my job helps carry out the vision of that company. But ultimately, I felt replaceable. It wasn't until I began fostering an intentional, intimate relationship with God that I learned that the unique role He has for me cannot be carried out by anyone else. He concocted this plan well before I was even born and chose to assign it specifically to me, giving me the option to choose if I'd like to participate or not. Isn't that wild to think about?

Do you remember how Paul talks about the body of Christ being made of many parts? You can find that whole passage in 1 Corinthians

12:12-27. That one chunk of scripture is alluding to the fact that we all have a unique role to play, and each one is vitally important to the ultimate goal of growing the kingdom of heaven and getting as many people into the Father's arms as we possibly can. I used to think that completely surrendering my life to Christ meant that I would have to go be a missionary in Uganda. I thought that that was the ultimate picture of righteousness and that every other job was just another tier under that one. The thing is, I didn't want to be a missionary. I have never had that desire ever in my life. Then when God showed me what my true identity in Him was, it changed everything. I wasn't being asked to uproot my life and move overseas. I was being asked to care for the people around me well and use my artistic abilities to carry out that task. That assignment was way more my speed.

The reason I'm telling you that story is because I don't want you to be afraid of finding your God-given identity. I don't want you to be concerned about everything you're going to "give up" but rather, everything you will gain. Don't get me wrong, there will be things you're going to have to sacrifice along the way, but you'll find that all of the things He has you release are things that we're weighing you down in the first place. Would you rather pull around an empty wagon, or a wagon full of junk? All He's going to ask you to do is throw out the junk a little at a time along the way. It may be anxiety inducing at times, sure, but the more you learn to trust Him, the more that will dissipate. You'll find that it actually makes the journey much easier as you go along. In Matthew 11:30, Jesus says, "For my yoke is easy and my burden is light." It's not about sacrificing everything you love so that you become a shell of your former self, it's about removing the weight you've accumulated over the course of your whole life so that you can run free again.

The reason why this concept seems so foreign to us is because the world around us has things completely backwards. Society tells us that we have to *do* something in order to *have* the things we need to *be* who we want to be. Whereas, in the kingdom of God, identity comes first. Once you know who you are in Christ, you have full permission to *be* that person. Then you *have* the tools to fulfill what it is that God is calling you to *do.* That's why we're called His beloved. We're designed to *be loved* before we move on to anything else. I once heard it said that identity comes before intimacy, intimacy comes before inheritance.[2] If you want everything that God has to offer you, you'll have to seek His heart before His hand. Seeking His heart also means that you will find yourself along the way.

One of my favorite movies of all time is *The Greatest Showman.* There's just something so satisfying about a misfit underdog weathering the storms of life and finding purpose and fulfillment in the most unlikely of places. One day, my friend[3] and I were discussing the song from that movie called "The Other Side." If you haven't seen the movie, this is the scene where Hugh Jackman's character is trying to convince Zac Efron's character to give up his elaborate lifestyle and join the circus. My friend pointed out, "He never promised that he wouldn't have to give anything up. In fact, he admitted that he would be giving up a lot. But the fulfillment he would get in return would be worth it." What a perfect picture of what it looks like to follow Jesus. You may think that you're giving up the things that make you happy when, in reality, you're only being asked to give up the things that keep you stuck.

So how do you find out what your individual identity is? How do you figure out what part you are in the body of Christ? I'll give you the same suggestion time and time again—you ask Him. Are you noticing a theme here? If you have a question, you ask God. It really is that simple, sometimes we just like to try and overcomplicate things with our formulas and rules. By now, you should be starting to get the hang of communicating with God, at least to the best of your ability. Take some time right now to ask Him how He sees you. Ask Him who you are to Him. Ask Him what He has for you. Then sit and listen until you get a response.

If you have a response, chances are you are now questioning that response. There's a good chance it sounds nothing like who you've always known yourself to be. That's because God doesn't see us in the way we currently present ourselves, He sees us as the person He originally created us to be, and He speaks to us as if we have already become them. Just look at King David. He was one of the most prolific kings in all of the Bible, and yet, he started out as a lowly shepherd boy that his own family didn't even consider for the chance to be the one anointed as king. Yet God considered him a king from the very beginning. Do you think David was ready and willing to step into that role? My guess would be no. In fact, there seems to be a point in his life where he runs from that calling. And yet with God's guidance and patience, he became the king he was always destined to be.

As you surrender yourself to God and begin to walk through the process of allowing Him to shape you into your created identity, it may be a little difficult at first. There's a good chance that nearly everything about you will evolve, right down to the way you carry yourself when you walk into a room. I remember a point in time when I looked into the mirror and was confused by what I saw. "God, I don't know her," I said. I was used to being this reserved, agreeable girl who spent far too much time being concerned with the way she was presenting herself to the world and always feeling like she was coming up short. I didn't like being that way, but it was familiar. It was all I had known for the first 30 years of my life. Over time, everything about me started to shift. I held my body up taller with my head high, I let go of the standards of outward perfection that I had clung to for so long. I began to dress differently, walk differently, and even interact with people differently. "I think I like her, but I don't know her," I repeated. The changes I was seeing in front of me were bizarre, but necessary.

My husband told me a story one time that put all of these compounding identity shifts into perspective. He said, "Did you know that juvenile bald eagles are nearly impossible to identify?" He began to explain that young bald eagles do not have the same plumage as their parents for about the first 5 years of their life, but over time, the feathers that they had been used to begin to shed, and they're replaced with feathers that resemble their father. Wow. What a word.

I want to encourage you to push past the self-doubt that will inevitably creep up because you're stepping into unfamiliar territory. I'm sure a caterpillar probably feels the same way the first time they stretch their wings as a butterfly. I remember the night before my first speaking engagement, I felt like a giant fraud. But the only reason I felt like a fraud was because I had never spoken on stage before. I frantically searched through my closet for just the right outfit. *What do speakers even wear?* I thought to myself. "Whatever you wear," God replied. Stepping into your identity is bound to be uncomfortable. But it's only because you're shedding parts of yourself that were never meant to be there in the first place.

Change can be difficult, especially if you're someone like me who finds comfort in predictability. And these changes won't happen overnight. Finding and stepping into your identity is a process. I'll add that, unlike the bald eagle babies, this process is optional for us. God isn't going to force you into the identity He wants you to have. He's a gentleman, and He will allow you the option to choose it for yourself. And if you choose this journey, at times, it's going to be very tempting to run back to what's familiar rather than stepping into these changes. Just remember that transformation happens as you go.

4

—— ⁕ ——

PURPOSE

At this point, we've reached the age-old question: "What is my purpose?" I think at some point in our lives, we've all wondered "Why am I here? What am I supposed to do with this life I've been given?" It's enough to send anyone into an existential crisis on a random Tuesday. The good news is that all of the work we've done over the last three days has been setting you up for success today. If you feel even a little bit confident that you have heard God's voice, been given an identity statement and a promise, discovering your purpose is a walk in the park. Seriously.

FINDING YOUR ROLE

You see, your purpose goes hand in hand with everything else we've learned. And you discover your purpose the same way you discovered everything else, by asking God. Honestly, if I had to summarize this book in three words, it would be really simple: Go ask God. I want to encourage you to do that right now. Take a little time to go ask Jesus what your purpose is, and then come back so that we can break it down even further.

I want you to think about these elements like a house. The ability to hear God's voice (along with scripture) is the foundation that you build your house on. The promises of God are the blueprints that give you the vision for what the end result is supposed to look like. Identity is the kind of house that it will be, such as a tudor, a craftsman, or even a castle. But the purpose is the framework that helps everything come together. Purpose consists of the day-to-day decisions that we make in order to bring the rest of this to fruition. So finding your purpose really isn't that difficult once you have the other building blocks in place.

MONEY'S ROLE IN YOUR PURPOSE

It seems as though a lot of us equate our purpose with success, and we equate success with money. Therefore, living out your purpose must mean you'll be successful and rich, right? Not necessarily.

> YOUR PURPOSE IS NOT DEFINED BY THE JOB YOU DO, THE MONEY YOU MAKE, OR THE SUCCESS YOU HAVE, IT'S DEFINED BY WHO YOU ARE AND WHAT YOU'RE CALLED TO DO.

So many of us get caught in the trap of trying to keep up with the Joneses because we assume that because they are wealthier, they must have found their purpose. Maybe if we do what they do and buy what they buy, we will find our purpose too. Stepping into your purpose isn't about competition, or about following in someone else's footsteps. Each person is going to have a purpose designed specifically for them. Some people are called to be stay at home parents. Some are called to be missionaries. Some are called to be teachers, pastors, or speakers.

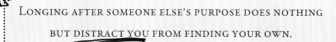

> LONGING AFTER SOMEONE ELSE'S PURPOSE DOES NOTHING
> BUT DISTRACT YOU FROM FINDING YOUR OWN.

There are some extremely wealthy people in this world who are absolutely miserable because their lives are devoid of purpose. They go around chasing fame, trying to stay relevant and investing in the next big thing. All the while, nothing seems to fill that gaping hole in their heart because nothing can, other than Jesus. It sounds corny, but it's true. On the other hand, I've known many people without a penny to their name who couldn't be happier because they are living out their purpose, which they understand isn't tied to their wealth. Now, I'm not saying that you have to be poor to find your purpose or that you can't find your purpose if you're rich. All I'm saying is that your unique purpose on this earth isn't tethered to your wealth, or lack thereof. It's attached to a sense of joy and fulfillment in knowing that you are doing exactly what you were put on this earth to do.

I used to think that money was the villian. Money was the one who turned people evil and made them greedy. It turns out, money was never the problem after all. It was people's hearts towards money that suckered them into those traps. 1 Timothy 6:10 says, "For the love of money is the root of all evil." The *love* of money, not money itself. I really had to shift my mindset on that one because I realized that I couldn't live a limitless life if I was locking myself into a certain tax bracket. What God showed me is that money is a *tool* that is designed to help you fulfill your purpose even more. If we look at ourselves as a funnel that money flows through into different projects and people, then we don't ever get attached to the money itself. This doesn't mean that God is opposed to you having nice things, however. He always gives good gifts to His children. And as one of my favorite pastors on the subject of money would say, "Even the inside of a hose gets wet."[1] Meaning that just because the money is flowing through you, doesn't mean some of it won't be for you, too.

There was a point in my life when I felt guilty about keeping any monetary gift God would give me. I felt like I had to give it all away because it would be selfish to keep it. Anytime I would have a little extra money in my account or get a payment that I wasn't expecting, I was constantly looking around for how I could bless other people with it. That wasn't a bad thing, but it was my heart that wasn't in proper alignment with what God wanted. He gave me a vision that I was a small child at my birthday party. God would hand me a gift and I would immediately turn around and pass it to one of the other children who were standing around me, watching. After about three or four passes, He finally stopped me and said, "I'm trying to celebrate *you*." He explained to me that although what I was doing was extremely kind and selfless, I was doing it because I didn't feel worthy of keeping those gifts for myself, even though He had picked them out just for me. God is not opposed to you possessing money, a new car, or quality clothes, He just doesn't want those things to possess you. They're simply tools to carry out your purpose, remember?

If money is a tool, then we have to invest the time into learning how to use that tool. Did you know that there are roughly 2,350 verses in the Bible pertaining to money? That means there is more than enough instruction in the Bible to teach you how to use the tools that are in your wallet right now. Study those Biblical financial principles, but don't forget to study the reasons behind them. Stewarding your money well isn't some list of rules that you follow so that God will bless you more, it's about learning to align yourself with the purpose that God wants that money to be used for. Tithing isn't something that you should think of like paying taxes to God so that you won't be locked in some sort of spiritual prison, instead, it's money that is specifically set aside for growing His kingdom. He once told me, "Give, don't pay. You are my daughter. Why would I make you pay for my favor?" Don't buy into the lie that tithing is some sort of exchange for God's favor. Instead, it's a way for us to use what He's already given us to get the word out about Him. As believers, we all want to see the kingdom grow. How cool is it that we get to play a part in that by giving a little bit of our paycheck towards such a big purpose?

STEPPING INTO YOUR PURPOSE

Stepping into your purpose is kind of like stepping into your identity. And, yes, much like owning your identity, discovering your purpose will take a little bit of time and a little bit of practice. Let's take a look at Queen Esther from the Bible. At first, she wasn't a queen at all, although God knew that that was her destiny and her unique identity. So before she could become queen, she had to undergo an entire year of beauty treatments. She likely became unrecognizable from her former self. It was a refining process, just like we talked about. Once her identity as queen was intact, she then had to walk in that purpose by caring for her people, even at the expense of her own life. Let's break it down.

Esther's Identity = Queen

Esther's Purpose = Lead and care for her people

Are you starting to see the difference? Your identity is a statement that helps you define who you are. Your purpose is how you live out that identity on a daily basis.

The sneaky part is, you're likely already familiar with your purpose on some level because, in most cases, it's linked to your unique personality. For example, I'm a sensitive person by nature. I've always had a tender heart for all living creatures, even some non-living creatures. I used to rotate the stuffed animals on my bed so that none of them would get their feelings hurt. Are you catching my drift? And so, when God called me to discipleship and teaching, it really wasn't that far-fetched of an idea. Because, although I am *not* a leader by nature, I know how to identify someone's pain and help them get free from it. It's like God takes the raw materials that are already in place, magnifies them and weaves them together in a way that we would never have thought of. Stepping into your purpose is as simple as using the materials He's already given you in the way that He intended them to be used from the beginning.

Sometimes, this takes discipline. It's not easy or effortless to find purpose in the boring things you have to do on a daily basis. This is why the Bible says we have to die to ourselves daily (John 11:25). That means that we have to set aside the things that we *want* to do and be disciplined enough to do the things we *need* to do in order to serve a greater purpose. For example, cleaning is not my favorite thing to do. I enjoy a clean house, I just don't necessarily love the effort that it takes to get it that way. But if I weren't disciplined enough to clean my house on a regular basis, then my family would be living in filth and that wouldn't be benefitting anyone. Walking in your purpose daily is not an easy task, I believe that's why Jesus said to take up our cross and follow Him (Matthew 16:24). Romans 8:17 says "we share in his sufferings in order that we may also share in his glory." If we want the glory of God to be evident in our lives, we can't just be fair-weather friends. We also have to go through the struggles that get us there. In my opinion, though, the glory is well worth it.

I'm reminded of that story in Acts 12. Peter has been imprisoned and an angel appears to bust him out of there. When the angel gets there, the first thing he tells Peter to do is to put on his shoes. You see, we can pray for divine intervention all day long. We can pray for God to show us the way and trust that He will. But ultimately, we are the ones who have to walk that path. The angel wasn't going to pick Peter up and carry him out of prison. It had to be an act of Peter's own free will. Unfortunately, some of us stay locked in the prison of our circumstances just because we're unwilling to walk out the freedom that God has for us. Put your shoes on, and I can promise you that you'll never want to go back.

I will caution you, however, that just as God can use your gifts for your benefit and His glory, the enemy can also use them for your destruction. God used my sensitivity as a tool to help me gain access to those around me who needed the love of Jesus. But before that, the enemy used my sensitivity to isolate and entangle me in a deeply-ingrained labyrinth of lies. Before I let Jesus take over my heart, I would overanalyze everything anyone said to me. I was able to pick up on the subtlest of cues that someone was frustrated with me and made it my life's mission to overcompensate for it which typically drove them away further. It was a vicious cycle that I couldn't seem to break because my own weapon was being used against me.

Have you ever been watching an action movie where the hero's enemy disarms them and points their own weapon at their face? You sit there defeated thinking, *He's toast. There's no way he will make it out of this one.* When all of a sudden, someone else shows up, whacks the enemy over the head, and saves the hero from certain destruction? Spoiler alert: that's exactly what Jesus wants to do for you. A lot of times, the enemy is pointing our own weapons at our face and we don't even recognize it. Doesn't that make you downright angry? Let me tell you the good news. Not only is Jesus going to rescue you from that hairy situation, He's also going to hand your weapon back to you, show you how to use it properly, and send you out into the battlefield where you're going to whoop some enemy tail. There's a battle cry rising up in your chest as you're reading this, I just know it. Let it out, my friend. It's okay if people stare.

The really exciting part is that you don't have to wait until you've fully transformed into your God-given identity to start living out your purpose. You don't even have to wait until your promises come true. There's no special moment where you have to "arrive" before you can lay hold of the fulfillment and passion that your purpose will bring. You can start living out your purpose right now, this very day, as soon as you discover it. Let's go back to the story of Joseph. Joseph had to wait a long time for his promises to come true. And although God had given him clues to point him towards his identity as a leader, it's difficult to step into that when you're living as a slave and as a prisoner. But that didn't mean that there was nothing for Joseph to do. He still walked in his purpose every single step of that journey. When he was a slave, he leaned into that responsibility and was put in charge of Potipher's house. When he was in prison, he stepped into responsibility there, moved up the ranks, interpreted dreams and helped others all the while. Those decisions were the framework that allowed him to step into his identity as a leader when the time was right. The execution of his purpose supported his promise. Just because you see the light at the end of the tunnel but aren't sure how to get there doesn't mean you have to wait for *someday* to enter into what God has called you to. That contentment and fulfillment is waiting for you right now. Doesn't that bring you a sigh of relief? That will surely make the waiting easier, won't it?

One thing I don't want you to do is overcomplicate your sense of purpose. Purpose is not something you're working towards, it's something you're living. We have a tendency to think of it as something that's attached to a day far into the future, when really it's in the mundane tasks of daily life. If you're a stay at home mom, even taking care of household chores can give you a sense of purpose. Think about it. If you're raising tiny disciples, then everything you do to invest in them is purposeful. Making sure they have clean clothes and full bellies is purposeful. Taking care of them when they're sick or won't sleep is purposeful. You may not see the fruit of that until far into the future, but that doesn't make it any less important right now. If you live your everyday life attaching everything you do to a greater purpose, that is where you find fulfillment.

I used to only want the big and exciting things that God had to offer me. I wanted the fireworks and the grand gestures. Then one day, my father-in-law said he felt like he had a word from God for me. *Yes, I thought, I love words from God. Bring on the fireworks!* He said, "God told me to tell you, 'Be faithful in the little things and the big things will come.'" Well, that was quite anticlimactic. Talk about taking the wind out of my sails. I was so focused on the extravagant things of God that I forgot that He's also in the smallest of details. It reminded me of the passage in 1 Kings 19:11-12, "Then a great and powerful wind tore the mountains apart and shattered the rocks before the Lord, but the Lord was not in the wind. After the wind there was an earthquake, but the Lord was not in the earthquake. After the earthquake came a fire, but the Lord was not in the fire. And after the fire came a gentle whisper." Don't get me wrong, God can show up in your life in big, magnanimous ways, but I've found that He teaches me more in day-to-day life than He ever has at a big event.

> SOMETIMES WHEN WE'RE SEARCHING FOR GOD IN EXTRA-
> ORDINARY THINGS, WE MISS HIM IN THE THINGS THAT ARE
> RIGHT IN FRONT OF OUR FACES.

Focus on finding the joy and the purpose in all of the little, mundane things and God will take care of the extraordinary.

WHEN PEOPLE COME AGAINST YOUR PURPOSE

Unfortunately, if you are walking in the path that God has for you, there are going to be people who come against it. Remember how I told you that the enemy likes to play teeter totter with us by simultaneously telling us that we're too much and not enough? Imagine it like there are two jars sitting in front of you, one big and one small. The small jar represents who society tells you to be and the large jar represents who God tells you that you are. Satan will try to convince you that you're too much for the small jar, causing you to shed parts of your created identity as you try to squeeze into it. But he will also tell you that you're not enough for the large jar. The truth is, you are exactly the right amount for everything that God has called you to be, but you have to bring all of the parts of your created identity to the table, including the parts that you shed along the way because you didn't believe that they belonged.

As sad as it is, when you throw the small jar away and commit yourself to that large jar, there are going to be people in your life who try to dig the small jar out of the trash and hand it back to you. Some people just are not comfortable with change, especially if that change causes you to be elevated and makes them feel less than because of their own insecurities. Don't compromise and don't shrink back, my friend. Instead, point them to the one person who can cause the same elevation for them.

Along those lines, not everyone in your life is going to be jumping up and down for you as you step into what God has for you. Do you remember when Jesus said, "A prophet has no honor in his hometown"? Jesus couldn't even perform miracles in his own home town because people only allowed themselves to see Him as the person He was before He stepped into His calling. This was one of the most difficult things for me to deal with as I started along my journey. There were certain people in my life, including friends and family, who were critical or even downright opposed to what I was doing. It hurt deeply, because they were the people that I wanted to come alongside me the most. As I do with all of my pain, I took it to Jesus. He said, "Caitlin, if your tree is bearing fruit, don't worry about the people who don't like apples." He was right. I had spent so much time focusing on the people who weren't being fed by the ministry God called me to than the people who were. Don't make the same mistake I did. Keep your eyes on the people who are ready and willing to be fed by your purpose.

In addition to a little opposition, you can expect that the enemy will send people who will try to tear you down and get you to question everything. I'm not going to sugarcoat this: it absolutely sucks, but you can't let it distract you from your purpose.

When I first started digging into discovering what my God-given identity was, I asked God to give me a few identity statements to hang onto. He gave me several, but the very first one seemed to stick out the most. The first thing He said was, "Honorable queen." Honorable queen? Me? The shy middle child sandwiched between two incredibly outgoing and charismatic siblings? The awkward kid who says "You too" whenever the waiter says, "enjoy your meal"? Me? Lead people?

HA! What a laugh. However, the more I thought about it, the more God brought to my memory story after story of how He used the most unlikely people to carry out the most important tasks. He spoke through Moses, the man with a speech impediment in order to save a nation. He honored an obedient prostitute by making her the great grandmother of the Messiah. He turned Saul from a judgemental murderer into Paul, one of the most influential evangelists of all time. Who was I to say that He couldn't possibly do the same in my life?

I reached a point where I started to catch the vision for my identity statement and see the seeds starting to bloom in my life. That is, until I came up against some toxic negativity that nearly cut me down at the root.

God had asked me to get on Tiktok and share what I was learning. As I did, my page began to amass quite a following very quickly. As I was using my voice to speak about the things that Jesus was teaching me, there were people who came in droves and started to tell me that what I was saying wasn't biblical, that I wasn't hearing from God, that I was a false teacher. You name it, I heard it. The thing is, there was a tiny bit of truth weaved within the fabric of those lies, which was what made it so easy to believe. I had just started studying the Bible in depth, who was I to teach people about it? I hadn't seen any evidence that the promises in my life would come to pass, who was I to prophesy that they would? I'm almost ashamed to admit that all of those lies nearly caused me to give up on that calling altogether.

One day in particular, I ran into my room, crying, pouring the entire contents of my heart out to Jesus. I told Him that I didn't know if I could do what He's asked me to do anymore. I told Him that I didn't think I was cut out for this, that maybe He chose the wrong person. Ever so gently, He reminded me of who I was. Who *He* said that I was.

"What is your identity?" He asked me.

I sniffled into my pillow and replied, "You called me an honorable queen."

"Yes," He said, "I told you that I would put a lot of people under your influence and that you would lead them well, and you have."

"But these other people are being so mean," I protested.

And that was when He hit me with the knockout punch. The coup de gras that broke the people-pleasing spirit right off of me. "A queen is still a queen no matter what the peasants say."

My tears instantly stopped flowing. I was so shocked by what I had just heard that my body seemed to dedicate all of its energy into digesting this one sentence. "God! Did you really just call those people peasants? I don't think you're allowed to do that." I heard a chuckle. "First of all, I'm God, and I'm allowed to do whatever I want. Second, listen to the meaning behind my words. A queen is characterized as someone who is rich and favored. A peasant is characterized as someone who is poor and desolate. You are rich in my presence and favored by my hand. You are a queen. Those people who claim to know so much about me don't spend any time with me. If they did, they would know better than to treat you that way. So I stand by what I said."

The moral of this story is that you will face all levels of opposition as you commit yourself to this path, but that doesn't mean that those people are right. Stay the course. Follow the way, the truth, and the life. And remember that a queen is still a queen no matter what the peasants say.

5

PEACE

Most of the time, we seem to think of peace as a life devoid of conflict or chaos when, in reality, you don't have to have a perfect life to achieve tranquility. You just have to chase after Jesus and you'll find peace as you find Him. Let's talk about the role that peace will play during your journey with God.

THE IMPORTANCE OF REST

Peace can often be associated with rest. If you think about the most peaceful place on earth, chances are you're going to choose somewhere where you would vacation rather than somewhere you frequent in your everyday life. A lot of times, we're chasing rest and chasing peace, treating it like a noun rather than a verb. Rest doesn't have to be achieved in certain places. Peace is not some flighty feeling that can be achieved after the business of life has quieted down. It's a fruit of the Spirit. So let's talk about how we can incorporate it into our everyday lives.

In the very first few chapters of the Bible, we can see that God Himself rested on the seventh day of creation. An infinite, limitless being chose to sit back and relax after all of His hard work. Why do you think that is? Do you think that He got tired? Did He use up all of His energy, or do you think that there's a possibility that He rested for another reason entirely? We'll get to that in a minute.

Throughout scripture, we see examples of people being commanded to rest. The sabbath day was set apart for that very reason. It's difficult for us to quiet our minds enough to let our bodies get a break. Sometimes, we have to be reminded. If you have children, then I'm sure you're all too familiar with the fact that kids love to fight their naps. Their little bodies need to rest because of all of the constant changes and growth that's happening within them, yet they're bound and determined to keep pushing through and neglect their rest entirely. Does that sound familiar? The good news is that God never asks us to do things that He isn't willing to demonstrate Himself. I can remember one day in particular where it felt like God had been extremely quiet. My human nature started to go through the mental checklist of everything that I possibly could have done wrong that would cause Him to pull away. Before I got done wracking my brain, that still, small voice quieted my fear. "I'm demonstrating rest," He said. I had been so used to running around like crazy trying to get things done that I neglected rest. And so, He reminded me what it was supposed to look like.

Over that next week, He revealed to me the importance of resting even in times of chaos. I was watching a video where this man was saying that one of the original Hebrew words for rest meant "to stop and take inventory." At that moment, something clicked in my brain.

REST IS A BATTLE STRATEGY.

It's no secret that we're all in a spiritual war. Ephesians 6:12 says, "For our struggle is not against flesh and blood, but against the rulers, against the authorities, against the powers of this dark world and against spiritual forces of evil in the heavenly realms." Think about an actual war. Wars are made up of battles, a smaller fight within a larger fight. After each battle, what do the troops do? They fall back, they get their bearings, they regroup, and they prepare for the next battle. It would look pretty silly if they went from battle to battle without taking the time to stop and strategize, wouldn't it? I'd venture to guess that they probably wouldn't win many battles that way, either.

Why do you think the devil is so bound and determined to make this world as busy as possible? If you don't take time to rest, you don't take time to think. If you don't take time to think, you don't take time to strategize against him. And if you keep that up for too long, you lose. By stopping to take inventory of where you've just come from, where you're going, and allowing God to give you the strategy to get there, you're setting yourself up for success. Trust me, rest is to your advantage.

PEACE STEMS FROM TRUST

Rest alone won't bring you undeniable peace. It will certainly help, but that's only part of the equation. The other part is about relinquishing control over your life. I have never considered myself to be a control freak, but I used to be a worry wart. As it turns out, worry is a form of wanting control. You want to be able to control the outcome of your circumstances and so you wrack your brain trying to think of ways to make your situation better. Does that sound peaceful to you? The presence of peace really stems from a lack of worry, and a total and complete trust that your Father will work everything out for your good.

Earlier, I mentioned our equine. One day, not too long ago, they escaped from their fence. We couldn't find them anywhere. We looked multiple times throughout the day and into the night. Finally, we realized there was nothing we could do. The weird thing was, I had complete and total peace. I trusted that they would come back, and I knew that even if they didn't, God would have a pretty good reason for allowing that to happen. In all honesty, the lack of worry made me feel a little bit cold-hearted. I used to equate worry with love. "I only worry because I really care," is what I would say. But the thing is, that worry did nothing but send me spinning in circles, chasing my own tail, and trying to find solutions to problems that never existed in the first place. But the peace that I had grown to acquire by trusting my Father, was a high I had never known before. Once you get a taste of that pure, unadulterated peace, no part of you ever wants to go back.

In order to understand what trusting God looks like, you first have to understand what it doesn't look like. I'm sure everyone has had a time in their life where they've said something to the effect of "I trusted God to heal that person and He didn't." Or maybe you trusted Him with a job, a relationship, or financial provision and He didn't come through like you thought He should.

> TRUSTING GOD DOES NOT MEAN THAT HE WILL HANDLE THE SITUATION IN THE WAY YOU THINK IT SHOULD BE HANDLED.

Isaiah 55:8-9 says, "'For my thoughts are not your thoughts, neither are my ways your ways,' declares the Lord.' As the heavens are higher than the earth, so are my ways higher than your ways and my thoughts higher than your thoughts.'" What this means is that God can see the bigger picture. So if He doesn't answer our prayers in the way that we think they should be answered, I promise you, He has a good reason.

My daughter is currently still a toddler, which means she loves to put shiny, colorful, round things in her mouth. I'm not sure why children have a habit of cramming choking hazards into their mouths, but they do. One thing she loves to play with when I'm not looking is her brother's marbles. We always try to keep the door to his room shut so that he can have his toys out without her getting into them. Every now and then, however, she wriggles her way in there and finds the marbles. Whenever I find her doing this, I remove her from the situation because I love her and I don't want her to get hurt. To her, that may seem a bit confusing. She may think *If you love me and want me to have fun, why would you take away something that makes me happy?* She doesn't see the dangerous situation that is looming every time she steps foot in the room with those marbles.

Sometimes, we have a tendency to do this with God. We read His word, so we get a better understanding of His will. We see that He says that He loves us, wants to prosper us and not to harm us, to give us hope and a future. (Jeremiah 29:11). Yet when we enter situations that look hopeless, we wonder why He isn't keeping His word. When we feel harmed by others, we wonder why He didn't intervene. When we're struggling and not prospering, we begin to question whether He even loves us at all. Have you ever been there? I want to encourage you that those emotions and those questions are perfectly normal. Just like I wasn't angry with my daughter for crying whenever I took her away from the marbles, God isn't mad at you for crying whenever you don't understand either.

> THE PURPOSE IS NOT TO UNDERSTAND EVERYTHING GOD
> DOES, THE PURPOSE IS TO TRUST THAT HE WILL WEAVE IT
> TOGETHER FOR YOUR BENEFIT EVEN WHEN YOU DON'T UN-
> DERSTAND.

I used to have a rottweiler named Bruce. He was arguably the best dog I have ever owned and, as an avid animal lover, I have owned *a lot* of dogs over the course of my lifetime. Bruce was so incredibly well behaved. He did absolutely everything I told him to, never chewed anything up, never peed on anything. He was just a big, loveable teddy bear that gained the affection of everyone he came into contact with. During the course of his life, he was my main source of comfort. He was with me through some very dark years and his gentle spirit helped guide me through it. If life felt overwhelming, I went to Bruce. If I needed a good cry, I hugged his giant neck and buried my face in his fluffy fur. If I was afraid, I sought him out for protection.

In 2019, Bruce was diagnosed with lymphoma and was gone just a few short months later. I was absolutely beside myself. I cried, I prayed, I begged God to let me keep him. And when Bruce didn't pull through, I was devastated. If God loves me, how can He take away something that brings me so much joy and comfort? I didn't find the answer to that question until a little over a year later when my father was diagnosed with stomach and esophageal cancer. Suddenly, Bruce was gone, my husband was out of town, and I was being forced to stare down the barrel of this diagnosis alone. Or so I thought. Because I had no other source of comfort, I was forced to look to God and God alone. Since that day, my whole life has turned upside down for the better. If I had still had Bruce in my life, I would have never had to lean on God for my strength. My life would not have been transformed. I would be the same timid, cowardly, anxious ball of nerves that I used to be. And you would most certainly not be reading this book right now.

My favorite verse in all of the Bible is Romans 8:28, "And we know that in all things God works for the good of those who love him, who have been called according to his purpose." *All things.* That means that loss works together for your benefit. Disaster and chaos work together for your benefit. *Everything* works together for your benefit when you have God on your side. When you can learn to turn over the control and trust that no matter what the outcome is, God will make it all work out by the end of your story, true peace is unlocked.

Before my daughter was born, I was perfectly content with my son. I knew that I wanted him to have siblings eventually, I just wasn't in a hurry to make that happen. I was enjoying the toddler stage with him and giving him my undivided attention. I used to joke that whenever it was time to have another baby, God was just going to have to tell me because I would likely never make that decision on my own. Little did I know, He was going to do just that. In the summer of 2020, I felt that tug on my heart that it was time to add another little one to our family. My husband and I decided to take a few months to think about it just to make sure. In late August, hurricane Laura hit. My husband, being an electrical lineman, was sent away to help with storm clean-up. Before he left, we made the decision that as soon as he got back, we would start trying for baby number two. While he was gone, my grandmother died, and the week of her funeral, my dad received his diagnosis. Needless to say, I did not feel that the timing of potentially expanding our family was ideal.

Whenever Josh got back, he told me that he was going to leave the baby decision up to me and that he was fine with whatever I decided. I told him he was going to have to give me a few days while I wrestled–I mean, prayed–to God about it. Every time I brought the subject to God, His response was always the same, "Do you trust me?"

When you're hit with a situation like that, you have to "put up or shut up" as they say. Meaning, if you say you trust God, now's the time to prove it. I want to make clear to you that I was absolutely quaking in my boots during the entire process of deciding whether or not to add another baby to our family, but I knew deep down in my gut that if I wanted to see what God was really all about, this was my chance to find out. It could go one of two ways: either it was going to turn out really good, or it was going to turn out really, *really* bad, but I knew that I would regret it for the rest of my life if I didn't take that leap.

Once we started trying, I got pregnant very quickly. I think that was God's way of making sure I wouldn't get cold feet. While that pregnancy wasn't easy by any stretch of the imagination, I believe my baby girl gave my dad something to fight for. If he didn't have the chance of meeting his granddaughter to look forward to, I'm honestly not sure if he would be here today or not. My dad told me later on that he had decided he was good with either outcome—whether he was going to stay here or God was going to call him home. He said he felt as though God was promising him more. He felt like this life had more to offer him. He told me he wasn't quite sure what that meant until he was holding Fiona for the first time. Then, he understood that "more" meant more time and enjoyment with his grandchildren and the rest of his family. "More" meant getting to meet her and watch her grow up. You ought to see them together now. You should see the way his eyes light up when she says, "Hi, Mott!" (because she can't quite pronounce Mac). You should see the way she shares her snacks with him and he pretends that it's the best thing he's ever tasted in his life. None of that would be possible without trust. No matter what you're going through right now, one day you'll be able to look back and see the purpose of it all. It's like that old quote, "If it's not good, God's not done." Don't throw the towel in early. Give God a chance to make it right. I know that it's a difficult concept, especially when things do not look like they're going to work out in your favor, but I can promise you this: If you are a child of God, He will *make* them work out in your favor.

PEACE UNDER FIRE

Let's address the elephant in the room. Because even if you're pressing into God, learning how to hear His voice, discovering your purpose and identity—the whole nine yards—you can expect one thing for certain. The enemy will come after you. That's because we have an enemy that is very emotionally reactive. At times, it may look like Satan has the upper hand. One thing we have to remember is that God is always playing the long game.

> GOD IS LOOKING FOR LONG-TERM WAYS TO BLESS YOU WHILE THE ENEMY IS LOOKING FOR SHORT-SIGHTED WAYS TO HURT YOU.

Now, I don't want you to be afraid, I want you to be equipped.

I used to love watching older movies with my mom. The movies weren't really that old, they just weren't intended for my generation. One of the ones we loved to watch was *Enough* starring Jennifer Lopez. The premise is that a domestic violence survivor escapes an abusive relationship. She decides that she is not going to be a victim anymore, so she concocts a plan to sneak back into this man's house and beat the tar out of him to ensure that he won't mess with her or her daughter anymore. This was a completely premeditated attempt that she even hires a trainer to help her carry out. During the course of her training, there is one scene in particular that always replays in my head whenever I'm under heavy spiritual attack.

Her trainer has her lay on the ground in order to simulate a situation where her abuser gets the upper hand. The trainer says, "He's standing over you. He thinks he's won. And as sure as he is a coward, he will try to kick you. But because you know what he'll do, you're smiling inside." You see, we don't have to be afraid of the enemy's attacks because we are preparing for them. We know that he will try to kick us while we're down, so we're prepared for how to handle it. For the rest of the day, I'll be your trainer, and you'll be Jennifer Lopez. Deal?

In order to know how to withstand spiritual warfare, you'll need to know how to use your weapons. Of course, you will have the voice of God to guide you, but that's only one tool in your toolbox. The enemy plays dirty and he doesn't take days off. In order to defend yourself from him, you'll need to make use of every weapon in your arsenal.

Using Your Sword

Your first weapon of defense should always be the word of God. If you don't have a physical copy of a Bible, get one. Read it every single day. This isn't a religious rule for you to follow, it's a sword that you're constantly sharpening the more you read. After Jesus was baptized, before He started His ministry, He was led into the wilderness for 40 days to fast and be tempted by the devil. Yet every single time the enemy tried to trap Him, even when Satan tried to use scripture against Jesus, Jesus had an understanding of the scripture that He unleashed like the weapon that it was. Because of His understanding of the written Word of God, His enemy couldn't stand. If you want the same victory, follow the same strategy.

A few months ago, I went through some of the most intense spiritual warfare of my life. God had really begun to move in my life and the enemy was *not* happy about it. He was coming after my mind in an intense way, trying to convince me that I didn't hear from God and that I was crazy. At the time, my husband was working nonstop as an electrical lineman, we had constant storms coming through our area so the kids and I couldn't really get out of the house, and our power kept going out. After a few days with very little sleep and no people around to speak truth into my life, I was actually starting to feel like those lies were true. I felt crazy. I felt like I had made it all up. I felt worthless.

Another storm rolled through and our power was knocked out again. I couldn't take another night of sleeping in the heat with two scared children and no help, so my husband convinced me to go spend the night at my in-law's house. By the time I got there, my husband had already called his parents to give them a head's up that I needed some encouragement. They sat me down and let me cry for an hour while I poured my heart out about how I felt. I had been pursuing God with my whole heart. I didn't understand why this was happening. I was reading all of the books, listening to all of the sermons, and absorbing all of the information I possibly thought would lead me closer to God. Ever so calmly, my father-in-law stood up and left the room. When he came back, he had his Bible in hand. He said, "Caitlin, this is your sword. Put down the books, put down the podcasts, and pick up your weapon." He pointed out that if I had been meditating on the Word of God, when the enemy tried to make me feel crazy, I could have easily counteracted it with scripture. 2 Timothy 1:7 (NKJV) says, "For God has not given us a spirit of fear; but of power, and of love, and of a sound mind." See? There was my smoking gun right there. If I had had that verse in my back pocket, I could've disabled the enemy's plan and stopped the whole attack in its tracks.

I understand that for a lot of people, the Bible can be incredibly confusing or, if we're really honest, even boring at times. You know what else can be kind of boring? Water. But you need it to survive. You've got to start getting the Word of the living water inside of you so that you can not only survive, but thrive. I realize that it can be difficult to even know where to start, so I want to give you a strategy on how to read and understand the Word of God, as well as apply it to your life.

I recently heard Jennie Allen describe her 3-step method for reading the Bible. Step one is to observe, step two is to interpret, and step three is to apply. I would throw an extra step in there and encourage you to pray before you ever read a single word. God can teach you anything at any time through any passage of scripture. Pray for Him to reveal something to you as you're reading, and open your Bible expecting Him to do just that. As you read, I want you to pretend that you are one of those actors in the *National Treasure* movies searching for hidden clues on the back of the Declaration of Independence. The clues are there, you just have to find them. Ask yourself questions like why things are repeated, why certain words or phrases are used and if there could be a deeper meaning behind them. When you get curious about what you're reading, you'll notice things that you've missed before that were right under your nose all along.

As you're asking these questions, it's super, super important to give Jesus time to answer you. Remember how we learned to hear His voice on day one? Don't just ask these questions to yourself, ask Him and let Him reveal the answers to you. He's not called "the teacher" for nothing. Once He's given you a deeper understanding about why these passages of scripture say what they say, you can now apply them to your everyday life. If you're not sure where to start reading, my personal recommendation is to start The Bible Recap. This reading plan takes you through the Bible in the order that the story unfolded, and offers deeper insights about what you're reading through their short, daily podcast episodes. It's a great way to not only make sure you're sharpening your sword everyday, but it also gives some thoughtful insights into the history and theology behind the scriptures.

Worship is a weapon

Another weapon you have at your disposal is worship. Simply putting on worship music and letting it play—even if you're not actively listening to it—changes the atmosphere. If you're feeling a heavy demonic presence in your home, just know that they hate the sound of people worshiping the one true God. Not only are you staking claim to God's territory, you're shifting your focus to Him who is bigger than any storm you could face in this life. That simple mindset shift can change your entire attitude for the rest of the day. This is a battle of the mind, after all.

A lot of us, whether we care to admit it or not, like to be in control. We like to have some sort of say over what is happening in our lives and it can be downright discouraging when things aren't going our way. Worship reminds us that there is a sovereign God who is working it all out for our good. It metaphorically takes us out of the driver's seat and puts us in the passenger seat where we belong. One thing about God is that He's the type of Father who will let you tire yourself out. You can worry yourself sick and He won't step in to stop you because, although He knows better, He wants it to be your choice whether you trust Him or not. Worship helps us remember who He is and make the right choices by surrendering our situations to Him.

Worship also shows our loyalty to God when times get difficult. If you can praise God for being good even when your situations are not, it displays that you are not just a fair weather friend, but that you are willing to stick with Him even when the going gets tough. Don't we all want people like that in our corner? We also want people in our corner who are going to hype us up before we go to bat for them, right? Remember that God has feelings too. He loves it when His kids encourage Him through worship by reminding Him how good we believe He is and how much we love Him. Have you ever played sports? If so, you've probably listened to some sort of music to pump you up before you get out there and face your opponent. If music changes our mood, encourages us, and motivates us, how much more excited do you think you would get if the songs were written about you and sung to you by the people you love the most. Now imagine how that must make God feel.

Have you ever done one of those science experiments where you use a mirror to reflect the sunlight and ignite a small fire? I want you to imagine worship like that. The mirror cannot start fires on its own, but it is reflecting the source of light that can. When we use our worship to angle God's goodness and point it at our situation, those circumstances become engulfed with the flames of His presence. That sounds like a pretty good way to win a battle to me.

The power of prayer

Finally, you have the weapon of prayer. Praying is simply inviting God to be involved in your life. Oftentimes, God will not step into your situation without your permission. Inviting Him in grants Him the opportunity to do some real damage to the kingdom of darkness. All you have to do is invite Him in, surrender control of the situation, and step out of the way while He delivers that knock-out punch.

When you think about it, prayer is essentially proof of your faith. Why would you pray if you didn't, to some degree, believe that someone was on the other side listening? It's one of the ways you exercise your faith by proving that you believe He is there. Now, that doesn't mean that He's going to answer us right away. Some people get so discouraged when they pray because they say things like "I didn't hear anything back" or "I prayed, but nothing happened." Just because we don't get an immediate response isn't because He isn't listening or doesn't want to talk to you.

My dad has a bad habit of not answering my questions right away. I can't tell you how many times I have asked him something only to question if he even heard me in the first place. He claims that he is contemplating his response, but sometimes I think he's actually doing that in order to force me to think about the question I just asked him. When Josh and I were dating, his dog had a large litter of puppies. I formed an instant connection with one of the puppies and was determined to bring him home, but I wasn't sure if my dad would go for it or not. When I finally worked up the nerve to ask him, we sat in silence for quite a while. In order to fill that silence, I started stating my case. I listed all of the reasons why I wanted this particular puppy and every responsibility that I was willing to take on in order to make it a smooth transition for everyone involved. My dad decided to let me keep the puppy. I think he knew that his answer was going to be yes from the beginning since he's as much of an animal lover as I am, but I think his pause in answering was so that I could contemplate how badly I really wanted it.

Unfortunately, sometimes the answer isn't always what we think it should be. Remember in the Lord's prayer when Jesus said, "Thy will be done"?

> PRAYER IS MORE ABOUT ALIGNING OURSELVES WITH GOD'S WILL THAN IT IS ABOUT BENDING HIM TO OURS.

We have to continually remind ourselves that God is a good Father who is acting in our best interests at all times. There's no formula for us to follow when we pray in order to get what we want. If my kids ask me for something, there are a lot of factors I take into consideration before I give them an answer. For example, if they ask for a snack, most of the time I will say yes because I don't want them to be hungry. However, if I know that we're about to eat dinner, my answer will probably be no because I don't want them to ruin their appetite. There is no formula that my kids can follow in order for me to give them a snack every time, without fail. All they can do is ask and then trust me to answer according to what I know is best for them. We have to choose to believe that God is doing the same for us.

Let me give you a personal example about a time when my prayers weren't answered the way I thought they should be. A couple of years after I lost Bruce, my rottweiler I mentioned earlier, I began praying for another companion dog. I prayed that prayer for nearly a year. Then, on Christmas morning 2022, after we had finished opening our presents and were getting ready to go to my sister's house, a dog showed up in our backyard. I heard God whisper, "My gift to you. I love you." That dog was an answered prayer. He was the fluffiest, friendliest companion dog who was always eager to please. We named him Chewy, which seemed to suit him because he would make a little growling noise like Chewbacca whenever he got excited. For two solid months, Chewy was my little shadow. He followed me everywhere and loved to be in my lap every chance he got, despite the fact that he was 65 pounds.

One day in February, just two short months after we adopted him into our family, he was hit by a car. We live on a dirt road in the middle of nowhere. I never anticipated that that would happen, especially to that dog, especially right after we got him. I just assumed that since God was the one who gave him to me, He would also be the one to protect him. I understood that sometimes accidents like this are the result of free will. Chewy chose to follow the other dogs into the road. The person who hit him chose to drive too fast and not to slow down when they saw the dogs. Sometimes, other people's choices cause a negative impact on our life through no fault of our own. There isn't always a direct correlation between the bad things that happen to us and our behavior. Just take the story of Job for example. Job was described as being upstanding and righteous, so much so that God was in heaven bragging on him. And yet, Job was hit with calamity after calamity, bringing chaos and destruction to his entire life. When his friends came around to "comfort" him, they essentially blamed him for his sorrow. If you're going through a really difficult time right now even though you've been doing your best, please understand that God isn't punishing you. Hard times happen to everyone, the righteous and unrighteous alike. God's love for you is not measured by your circumstances.

The thing is, at first, it seemed as though Chewy would be alright. His leg was obviously broken, but he was able to hobble around on the other three and make his way to me so that I could load him into the car and take him to the vet. On the way there, I thanked God for his life, thanked Him for giving Chewy to me, prayed for his healing, and declared life over his body. By all intents and purposes, I did everything right. That should have worked, right? Only it didn't. Just a few hours later, he went into cardiac arrest on the table at the vet's office. Talk about devastation. For an animal lover like me, that was worse than a shot to the heart. I thought that if I prayed the right prayer or claimed healing and used my faith, that that would work.

For days, I was angry with God. I couldn't believe that He would give me such a beautiful gift only for it to be snatched away such a short time later. It seemed so cruel. I hadn't known God to be cruel before, but that was one of those situations that I just couldn't seem to understand. If He was all powerful, couldn't He step in to save my dog's life? If He loved me, wouldn't He want to ease my pain? After I poured all of my feelings to God over the course of several days, I finally heard the words, "What if I spared you from a worse fate?" That question really caused me to stop and think. I hadn't considered it from that angle before. He continued, "Whenever you pray all of the right prayers and say all of the right things and I still don't answer the way you want me to, just know that I have a good reason for that." To this day, I still don't understand why Chewy had to go. I may never understand on this side of heaven. But I'm able to rest in the fact that my Father is acting in my best interests, even if I can't see evidence of that in my circumstances. My prayers may not have changed my circumstances but because I was constantly crying out to God, those prayers changed my heart.

Four kinds of prayer

Now that you understand the purpose of prayer a little bit better, I want to dive into the different kinds of prayer[1] and the purpose that each of them serve. The four basic kinds of prayer are conversational prayers, intercession, bold prayers, and praying in the spirit. It seems as though a lot of people get stuck sticking to one kind of prayer, not realizing that other types of prayer serve different purposes. Let's break them down.

Conversational prayer is just what it sounds like: a conversation. This is the kind of prayer that I covered on day one. You bring your worries, concerns, victories, questions and requests to God and allow Him to answer you. This is the kind of prayer that builds up your relationship with Him and helps you get to know Him a little bit better. It's essentially like having a standing coffee date with God every time you pray.

Intercessory prayer is more about praying on behalf of another person. This seems to be the type of prayer that most Christians adopt as their main form of communication. It may sound something like this: "God please be with my friend. She's going through a hard time right now. Please give her peace as she walks through this hard situation." In intercession, you bring your requests to God and expect Him to move as a result. Even though the example I just gave was a quick one, there's nothing casual about intercession. You are quite literally going to war for someone else. You're offering to stand in the gap between your friend and your Father and bring them together all while intercepting the very evil that is trying to destroy them. That kind of privilege should not be taken lightly. While this type of prayer is *vital,* we cannot lean on it as our only form of communication with God. How would you like it if you had a friend who only contacted you whenever they wanted something from you? That wouldn't be much of a friendship, would it?

Bold prayers are the type of words that start forming on your lips once you learn the will of God for your life. These are declarative statements that you utter in order to command your situation to get in line with God's will. If you know that God's will is for you to be healthy, you may make a remark that sounds something like this: "In the name of Jesus, I command my body to be healthy. By His stripes, I am healed!" That is a bold prayer. Think about this: if we are made in God's image, that means we create the way God creates. How does God create? With His words Genesis 1:3 says, "*And God said,* 'Let there be light,' and there was light." God spoke, and it appeared. If we are made in His image and have been given authority, that means that our words have power. That doesn't mean that your words and your feelings will always align.

> SOMETIMES YOU HAVE TO SPEAK LIFE INTO THINGS BEFORE
> YOU EVER SEE THEM GROW.

This also means that the enemy is after your words. He does not have the power to create, only to imitate. In order for him to be able to create something, he has to borrow your power by getting you to agree with him with your words. There is power in agreement. If you declare with your mouth that you'll never get ahead on your bills, then you are speaking that into existence. You've just given the enemy permission to use the power that God gave you to create. Just as a side note, one way that the enemy gets you to verbally agree with his agenda is through the lyrics you sing. Be careful what you listen to, and pay attention to what you say. If you start speaking life into your body, into your marriage, into your children and into your situations, I can guarantee that you will eventually see those actions bear fruit.

The final type of prayer is praying in the spirit. Being unsure of what to pray is a completely normal conundrum that a lot of people face. I faced it myself the night my father was diagnosed with cancer.

I had no idea what to say or how to pray for him, I just knew that I couldn't stop praying. I couldn't give the enemy a single inch to wiggle his mangey claws in there and take hold of things. I had to keep praying, but what was I supposed to say? I asked God to grant me the ability to pray in tongues, just like the church did in Acts when they were all filled with the Holy Spirit. You see, I had ignored the Holy Spirit for so long because I didn't really understand His role. But that night, I remembered that He was often referred to as the Comforter and the Guide. I surely could have used some comfort and guidance at that point. So I sat in that chair in my living room, waiting for something to happen. Then, I figured that if I was going to ask for the ability of tongues, I should open my mouth as a sign of faith that He would grant my request. As soon as I did that, the words came flowing out of me.

At the time, I didn't quite understand what I was doing, I just knew that there was power behind it. I knew that 1 Corinthians 14:2 said, "For anyone who speaks in a tongue does not speak to people but to God." So I knew that I was essentially giving the Holy Spirit permission to talk to God on my behalf. Why would He need our words to do that? Because our words are powerful. Our words are what we use to create. It would only make sense to allow the Holy Spirit to use my words to communicate the perfect prayers to the Father. I knew that speaking in tongues was a way to get my mind and my will out of the way and get into alignment with the perfect will of God. I understood that it was a way to pray when we didn't seem to have the words (Romans 8:26-27), but I wanted a bit more of an explanation. So, naturally, I asked God to explain it to me. This was the example He gave me:

"Let's say you go to a baseball game. You're so excited to watch your team play and you really want them to win. As you're watching, the catcher motions for you to come to him on the field. When you get down there, he says, 'Hey, kid. You want to help us win this thing?' Your eyes light up because you can't believe you get the chance to participate in something so special. The catcher begins to show you the secret hand signals that he and the pitcher use to communicate about what pitch will be thrown. You begin to use these hand signals to communicate with the pitcher, and he decides on a pitch. You have no idea what those hand signals mean and neither does the opposing team. But the pitcher does and the catcher does and that's all that matters. You're just happy that you got to help your team win."

When you think about it that way, it seems kind of surreal that God would even let us play a part in all of this. But that's how much He loves you. Praying isn't so that He will bend to your will and do what you ask, it's so that you get to play a part in helping your team win the game. And knowing that you're a part of something larger than yourself and the situations you're currently facing is a breeding ground for the peace of the Lord to envelop you.

PEACE WITH OTHERS

Whether we like it or not, at some point in our lives, we have to learn how to get along with others. I realize that sometimes other people make this extremely difficult, but that doesn't make this task any less important. We were designed to need each other.

Did you know that trees live in communities? I love how nature points us to the way God originally designed things. Above ground, these trees may look like they are all living independently of each other, but if you dive beneath the surface, you'll find that their roots connect together to form a neural network much like the nervous system found in our bodies. When one tree is sick, the other trees will send it extra nutrients to care for it until it's healthy again. When seedlings sprout, the mother tree is able to recognize her offspring and produce a sugary substance that sustains the saplings life until it's old enough to reach the sunlight on its own. While the mother tree is depleting her own nutrients by feeding her offspring, the rest of the trees are making sure she has enough nutrients to support her own health. They are even able to warn each other of danger by releasing gasses into the air that send signals to the other trees to act in a way that will protect them. They either make their leaves bitter so that no animals will want to strip them of their leaves, or they release pheramones into the air that will attract animals and insects that will protect them. Fascinating, isn't it? If trees can instinctively know how to live in community so well and take care of each other, I think we as humans can probably figure it out, don't you?

The good news is that this is clearly outlined for us in scripture. Remember how we talked about the body of Christ? That not only points to our roles and responsibilities, it also points to community and how we are intended to work together. While we're in such close proximity with other people, there's bound to be conflict at one point or another because we are working directly with imperfect people. At one point or another, I believe most of us have experienced some level of church hurt. While that's not at all how it was designed to happen, it's a good thing Jesus saw this coming and pointed us towards the solution in Matthew 18:15-17 (NLT):

> "If another believer sins against you, go privately and point out the offense. If the other person listens and confesses it, you have won that person back. But if you are unsuccessful, take one or two others with you and go back again, so that everything you say may be confirmed by two or three witnesses. If the person still refuses to listen, take your case to the church. Then if he or she won't accept the church's decision, treat that person as a pagan or a corrupt tax collector."

There are several things we can learn from this short passage. First, we learn that Jesus doesn't want us to be passive aggressive in the way we handle conflict. He calls us to be direct in squashing the issue at hand. By going directly to the person who has offended us and pointing out the offense, it gives them the opportunity to talk things out and explain their side.

When my husband and I first started dating, I had a really bad habit of lying in order to spare his feelings. I learned very quickly that he was not a fan of that approach. At one point he told me, "I would rather you tell me the truth even if it hurts me than tell me a lie to spare my feelings and destroy my trust." He taught me early on that the truth is absolutely necessary in relationships, especially when it's uncomfortable or even painful. Most of us have a tendency to think that we shouldn't be open and honest with people because we believe that risking hurting someone's feelings is not in line with how God calls us to be kind and loving. I want to challenge you on this. Placating someone's feelings is not loving, it's coddling. God never called us to coddle anyone, He called us to speak the truth in love.

Did you know that although the Bible instructs us to be kind over four-hundred times, it never once instructs us to be nice. Kindness is defined as "the quality of being friendly, generous, and considerate" while nice means to be "pleasant, agreeable, or satisfactory." Let me reiterate this: It is not your job to be agreeable, it is your job to be considerate. So many of us have been snared in the trap of people-pleasing at some point or another, myself included. We tend to believe that in order to be kind to others, we have to bend over backwards and re-shape everything about ourselves in order to cram ourselves into the molds that other people think we should fit. One day, God pointed out to me that people-pleasing is essentially an inconsistency in character. God's character is absolutely unchanging. If we want to emulate Him, we need to be willing to follow His example. If we are constantly shifting the way we present ourselves depending on who is around, then nobody is able to easily pinpoint who we are and what we stand for. If we stand for truth and stand for the Word of God, there are going to be people who don't like it. And yes, some of those people will even be fellow Christians. Regardless of the way people perceive us, we are called to stand firm, because we do not build our houses on shifting sand, but rather on the Rock of Ages. (Matthew 7:24-26).

Another thing we learn from that passage is that although we may make multiple attempts to mend a relationship, sometimes there will be people in our lives who will be unwilling to mend things. I used to get so bent out of shape when people would exit my life. There was an entire period of my life where I lost friendship after friendship. I largely blamed myself because I seemed to be the only common denominator. I'm the type of person who pours my heart and soul into the people I love, so watching those people walk right out of my life like

I never existed was extra devastating. And while there were definitely things that I could have done differently in order to work things out with others, God gave me a different perspective on the matter. He told me, "You are a safe harbor. People come to you to refuel. You give them what they need physically, spiritually, mentally, and emotionally. But ships weren't meant to stay in the harbor forever. Sometimes, you have to let people continue their journey without you." Sometimes people leaving our lives has absolutely nothing to do with us, we just weren't meant to be in their life long-term, and that's okay.

While some people leave our lives voluntarily, there are always those tricky relationships where you have to still cohabitate with them in some form or another. What does Jesus say about those situations? That last sentence in the above passage where it says to "treat them as a pagan or a tax collector" is interesting to me. Do you know how they treated tax collectors back in the day? They didn't hang out with them. They didn't eat dinner with them, they didn't socialize with them, they kept all interaction with them to a bare minimum, only speaking to them when necessary. They still had to interact with tax collectors from time to time for the purpose of business, but they didn't go out of their way to extend their friendship.

It always baffles me when people think that God isn't okay with us setting boundaries. As if boundaries are somehow unkind. There was a time in my life when my relationship with someone I was close to was in hot water. God had promised me that He was going to restore that relationship, but I was struggling to figure out how He wanted me to navigate interactions with them while I waited. One day as I was overthinking about it, He gave me a vision. In this vision, there was a person sitting in a chair with an injured leg. I was tending to their wound, cleaning it, disinfecting it, and bandaging it for them. I said to them, "The doctor is on the way. Until He gets here, I'm going to get you some pain medicine, dress your wound, and make you as comfortable as I can." I scoffed. *You mean I'm supposed to cater to this person's every whim while I wait for you to fix this?* He took me back to the vision and showed me who was sitting in the chair with the injured leg. It was me. "It's okay to take care of yourself until I fix this," He said. Having faith for God to restore your relationships doesn't mean that you have to injure yourself further while you wait. Proverbs 4:23 says, "Above all else, guard your heart, for everything you do flows from it." If you're allowing your heart to constantly be injured by others, it hinders your ability to love other people properly. It clouds your judgment because you're operating from a wound rather than operating from a place of peace. I firmly believe that God is okay with boundaries, so long as they are carried out correctly.

How do you implement appropriate boundaries? I once heard it said that boundaries are not about controlling the other person's behavior, they're about communicating what *you* will do if a certain behavior pattern of theirs continues. I've been trying to teach my son about appropriate boundaries. My daughter is in a phase where she likes to hit or throw things whenever she's frustrated. Whenever she hits her brother, he comes to me to seek instruction on what to do. Of course, I try to teach my daughter not to hit or throw, but I also try to teach my son that he has permission to communicate that he is not okay with her behavior. I tell him, "If your sister hits you, you tell her that that hurts and ask her to stop. If she hits you again, walk away." In that scenario, my son is not controlling his sister's behavior. Instead, he is taking action that protects himself from getting hurt any further. That is what appropriate boundaries look like. It doesn't mean that you have to cut someone out of your life entirely, it simply means that you implement self-control in the way that you respond to their behavior. Self-control is a fruit of the Spirit, after all.

In addition to boundaries with people who have hurt you, it's also important to be mindful of the people with which you surround yourself. I used to have a bad habit of hanging out with anyone who wanted to hang out with me. Maybe it was my fear of rejection, but I just went into friendships thinking that I was the weaker link and these kind souls were somehow showing me pity by extending their friendship. I gladly accepted the offer every time. It took me a long time to learn that not everywhere that I was invited was where I belonged. There were plenty of good-hearted people in my life who were more of a distraction than anything.

> LOVING OTHERS AND CREATING COMMUNITY DOESN'T
> EQUATE TO SACRIFICING YOUR STANDARDS.

Jesus loved everyone, and yet He only surrounded Himself with twelve men on a regular basis.

My best friend, Brenda, and I went out for coffee one day. We were laughing about the fact that it's so hard to make friends as an adult. I made the comment that I only felt like I had one or two friends to share my life with. She said the same. I laughed and made the remark that we were a little pathetic. A puzzled look crossed her face. "Why do you say that?" she asked. "Well, because I feel like we should have a bigger sense of community, don't you?" I replied. Her response has been ringing in my ears ever since I heard it. "Not necessarily," she said, "I only surround myself with the people I admire. If that means my circle is small, then so be it." What a profound way to look at life. It is true that the people you surround yourself with have a massive impact on your life. Eagles only tend to hang out with other eagles. Why? Because if they were to form a friendship with a bear, that bear would never be able to fly, which means the eagle would always have to sacrifice their potential in order to maintain that friendship. Some people aren't willing to grow to their full potential. Surround yourself with people who allow you to fly.

FORGIVENESS

You cannot have peace without forgiveness. I'm sure you've heard the saying "unforgiveness is like drinking poison and expecting the other person to die." We all know that forgiveness is important and even necessary in theory, but it can be a tough concept to carry out. For most of us, unforgiveness can feel like a righteous punishment for the other person. As if releasing them from that punishment would somehow be letting them get away with what they've done. We treat those situations as if it's almost necessary to harbor resentment as a way to warn others that those people are untrustworthy. Believe me, I used to be the world's worst at holding grudges. I believed that every harmful action deserved an apology. That kind of thinking wasn't necessarily wrong, but it wasn't reality either. The truth is, when you're dealing with imperfect people, most of the time you won't get an apology. Most of the time, they are unaware that what they've done is even wrong, or they're finding some way to justify their actions to themselves. So how do you let go of that? How do you just let people treat you poorly and then let it go?

I never really understood why forgiveness was so important until one day, God gave me a vision. Everyone who had ever hurt me was locked behind a gate. *As they should be,* I thought. All of a sudden, the gate flew open and everyone that was previously locked away escaped. They were running as fast as they could in different directions. *Great,* I thought, *now they're free to go hurt other people.* All of a sudden, a light exploded from inside the gate like a supernova. It knocked all of the people who had just escaped flat on their faces. When they got up, they were glowing with the same light that had just leveled them moments before. Now, they weren't running out into the world to hurt other people, they were going to spread the light.

In Luke 7:47, we see Jesus teaching that those who are forgiven much, love much. There is no greater way to show someone the love of Jesus than to forgive the person who has never apologized. Do you remember the parable of the unforgiving debtor? You can read all about it in Matthew 18. Jesus tells this story after Peter asks Him how many times he's supposed to forgive someone. Peter was probably thinking, "Come on, Jesus, be reasonable!" We've all had that thought pattern at some point or another. In this parable, Jesus tells the story of a man who owed a large debt to the king. After the man begged for mercy, the king forgave his debt. Immediately, this man leaves the king's presence and goes to hassle everyone who owed him money. How ridiculous, right? And yet we've all behaved like that man in some way, shape, or form when we tuck unforgiveness away in our hearts.

Go back and take a quick look at the Ten Commandments. Can you honestly say that you've kept all ten of those commandments for your entire life? Of course you haven't! You're human, after all. Because we have all sinned, we deserved death. Eternal death. But God forgave us. He loved us so much that He chose not only to show us mercy by sparing us the punishment, but He loves and honors us by adopting us into His family (if we agree to it) and forgetting every mistake we've ever made. Try and wrap your head around that for a minute. If God can forgive us and then turn right around and give us honor, what makes us think we can't at least release the people we have locked behind that gate?

I understand how difficult it is. Trust me, I have been betrayed in some of the worst ways you can imagine, and yet I can honestly say that I don't hold an ounce of unforgiveness in my heart towards those people. Do you know how that makes me feel? Free. I'm no longer chained to the people who did me wrong. I can go months at a time without ever thinking about them, and when they do get brought up, they are but a fleeting thought or a brief memory. It's all because I severed the cord that tethered me to them. Sometimes the people who have hurt you are people that you still have to be in contact with on a regular basis. I know how difficult that can be. But I want you to imagine for a minute that the next time you walk into the room with that person, your mood is unaffected. Imagine being able to walk past them without giving them the power to push your buttons. How much better would that make you feel? How much anxiety and tension would that remove from your life? Are you sure you still want to hold onto that resentment? Or have I started to convince you that maybe, just maybe, it's worth it to let it go?

6

— : —

INTIMACY

Sometimes people will associate intimacy with a physical connection, so it can get kind of confusing for them to understand how we're supposed to have intimacy with Christ. I once heard a preacher[1] describe intimacy with God as "into-me-see." It's less about a physical act of expression of our love and more about laying our hearts bare at the feet of Jesus so that He can work in our lives and clean up all of the junk.

CONSTANT COMMUNICATION

Sometimes I hear people ask, "Why do I need to tell God anything if He already knows everything?" That's a great question. If the only reason we told God anything was to relay information, we wouldn't have to tell Him anything at all. However, our communication with God is more about establishing a close relationship with Him.

Let me give you an illustration to paint this picture a little better. Let's say you're a teenager. You sneak out one night to go to a party. While you're at this party, you partake of a few adult beverages and get into a fender bender with a nearby tree on the way home. Little do you know, your buddy told his mom what happened and his mom called your mom. Your mom already knows what happened, but she hasn't heard it from you. Guilt and shame from your actions may tempt you not to tell her. Fear of discipline may cause you to keep that information to yourself. But in all reality, your mom loves you and wants to help you. She wants to guide you through the right way to handle this situation so that you don't have to go through anything like this again. But if you don't willingly come to her and open up to her about how you're feeling about what took place, she's very limited in her ability to help.

It's the same thing with God. Of course He already knows. He knows everything that will ever happen over the course of your entire lifetime, but He still wants to hear it from you. I'll be honest, I really used to struggle with this too. I carried a lot of shame as a child. The enemy tried to convince me that I needed to be perfect. I was already a rule-follower by nature, so whenever I broke a rule, it felt like the end of the world. It didn't take much for the enemy to convince me I was worthless. Because of that, my relationship with Jesus was stifled. You see, I accepted Jesus into my heart when I was about eight years old. But because of the level of shame I had buried deep inside, I only let Him into the foyer of my heart. I got Him a nice chair, welcomed Him in, and told Him to sit there and not wander around too much because there were things I didn't want Him to see. And because God is a gentleman, He honored my wishes and sat in that chair for 23 years. Then one day, I came running into the room and said, "I need your help. My dad has cancer. I'm scared and alone and I don't know what to do." It was as if His response was, "Okay. Do I get to come all the way in now?"

It was at that moment that I let Him come all the way into my life. I allowed Him to see all of the shame and guilt I had been hoarding for decades. And like a professional organizer, He began to clean the place up, keeping the things that were important and tossing the things that were holding me back. Allowing Him into the depths of my heart allowed me the freedom to breathe again. Suddenly, I didn't have to bear those burdens alone. In fact, I didn't have to carry them at all. Matthew 11:28-30 says, "Come to me, all you who are weary and burdened, and I will give you rest. Take my yoke upon you and learn from me, for I am gentle and humble in heart, and you will find rest for your souls. For my yoke is easy and my burden is light." Jesus swapped yokes with me that day. I want that same freedom for you, but that means you have to allow Him all the way in.

You may say, "Well, how do I even do that?" The answer is simple: you bring *everything* to Him. No secrets, no pleasantries, no skirting around the issue and giving Sunday School answers. Bring your honest feelings, your raw heart, your deepest pains to Him whenever you spend time together. A little while ago, we had a coyote attack our chickens and kill almost all of them. It was like losing 27 pets at once. I was absolutely devastated. I could not seem to stop crying. I kept looking to God to comfort me, but every time I spent time with Him, I would just spend the whole time crying. I finally said, "God, I'm so tired of crying." When He asked me why, I told Him it was because it left me feeling so drained and depleted every time I would cry that much. His response was, "You have to be drained so I can fill you back up."

I'm sure you've heard the phrase "You can't pour from an empty cup." I would agree that that's true, however I would encourage you to examine what or who you are turning to in order to fill your cup. If you're turning to self-care tactics to fulfill you, you might be putting a bandaid on a bullet wound. If you're turning to other people to reassure you and uplift you, that codependency is setting you up for failure whenever those human beings inevitably make a mistake. However, if you are looking to God as your source, your cup will never run dry again. John 4:13-14 says, "Jesus answered, 'Everyone who drinks this water will be thirsty again, but whoever drinks the water I give them will never thirst. Indeed, the water I give them will become in them a spring of water welling up to eternal life.'" It reminds me of that old saying, "If you give a man a fish, he will eat for a day. If you teach a man to fish, he will eat for a lifetime." We have to remember that God is playing the long game. He's not interested in short-term solutions. Everything that He does is done with excellence, sometimes it just requires us to be willing to undergo the process.

Whenever we change the water in our horses trough, we have to fully drain it. Usually, it's full of leaves and mosquito larvae and other things we don't want our horse to drink. So we drain the trough completely, rinse it out to get rid of any residue that may try to cling to the sides, and fill it back up with fresh, cool water. That fresh water replenishes the animals and keeps them healthy so that they have the energy they need to go about their day. So how do you create intimacy with God? Go to Him and drain the trough. Get all of the yucky stuff out of you. Tell him all of your worries, fears, feelings of anger and resentment. *Drain it all.* Then sit in His presence long enough for Him to fill you back up.

INVITE GOD INTO EVERY SITUATION

We've already discussed how you should bring all of your thoughts and feelings to God, but I don't want you to stop there. Imagine you had a friend who only called you when they needed something from you or wanted to complain. That wouldn't be much of a friendship, would it? That's why it's just as important to invite God into the good times too. You got a promotion? Great! Celebrate with God. Your kid just took their first steps? How exciting! Stop and take a minute to thank God for giving you that child in the first place.

Spending intentional time with someone is one of the most important steps in fostering any healthy relationship. It's no different with God. There was a season of my life where I would stay up after my kids and my husband were in bed so that I could spend about an hour each night talking to God. During that time, I wasn't getting out my Bible or listening to worship music (although you could absolutely do that, too). Instead, I was asking Him questions, asking Him to teach me things, and getting His opinion on certain situations. That one year of my life radically shifted everything. Over time, I got to know my Father because I had spent intentional time in His presence seeking His heart. During that one season, He taught me everything you are reading about in this book. Just think of all of the things He could teach you if you devoted a little bit of time to getting to know Him better.

A friend of mine[2] likes to take that idea a step further. She developed a habit of going on dates with God. She gets dressed up, leaves her kids in the care of her husband, and goes somewhere to spend intentional time with God. It could be a walk through the park, it could be getting ice cream or going to dinner. It doesn't matter what she does, it matters who she is spending time with. Will you feel crazy or look a little silly at first? Yeah, probably. But I would challenge you to try it anyway and see if it makes a difference in your life. God is a very intentional, very relational God. He doesn't just want your best efforts and He doesn't just want your struggles. He wants every single solitary part of you. The messy parts, the hard parts, the good times and the celebrations alike. It's up to you to give it to Him.

Of course, intimacy does require vulnerability. I know that is a tricky subject for a lot of people. Over time, we've developed these fences around our hearts and walls around our lives so that no one can see us struggling. We've been conditioned to believe that we must present a nearly perfect version of ourselves in order to be accepted, and sometimes that wrong thinking trickles into our relationship with God. Trust me, there is nothing that you can do to scare God away. There is nothing you could say to Him and nothing that you could confess to make Him love you less. He already knows all of it and has chosen you anyway. But that level of vulnerability is what is going to reel you closer to His heart. It's time to stop playing games with God, my friend. Let those walls down, bust holes in those fences and bring Him your raw, honest heart.

Whenever I say that you should constantly be spending time with God, I don't just mean whenever you are feeling religious. I mean to quite literally invite Him into every situation, especially the ones that you couldn't see Him in before. I once heard Him instruct me to do a sewing project for somebody. He wanted me to make a blanket inspired by the line "Who told the ocean you can only come this far?" from the song "My Redeemer Lives". I had a lot of scrap fabric, and so I designed an idea for a quilt that would look like ocean waves meeting the shore. As I sat down to sew this blanket, I was really struggling to sew the angles together correctly in order to form the pattern I wanted. Geometry was never my strong suit. After several attempts, I almost gave up. Then I heard that still, small voice that I had become so familiar with. "Connect the largest angle at the bottom of the fabric and the smallest angle at the top," He said. I tried it, and it worked. I couldn't believe it. I had known to pray about situations that were outside of my control, but I had never thought about praying for Him to teach me something practical. But why shouldn't He be involved in that? He created the person who invented sewing, after all. In fact, He created the person who invented geometry. There is quite literally nothing He cannot teach you when you are open and willing to learn.

The coolest part of that story was that I had no idea who would be getting this blanket. He had asked me to include a pink starfish, so the first person I thought of was a long-distance friend who was struggling with infertility. Maybe He would ask me to send it to her as a sign of hope to not give up on getting pregnant. I finished it up the day before the deadline He gave me. He then gave me a picture in my head of a woman I didn't recognize. She had short, salt and pepper hair, cut above the ears and wore dark-rimmed glasses. What was I supposed to do with that information? How was I supposed to find her? His instructions were clear: "Keep the blanket with you. Go about your day and you will see her."

The next day at church, I saw that same woman on stage, singing with the worship team, wearing a pink shirt with stars on it. That was too much detail to be a coincidence. I didn't recognize her because she had just cut her hair short above the ears, just like the picture in my mind. She normally attended a different service than I did, so I hadn't had much chance to interact with her.

After she left the stage, I intercepted her in the lobby to give her the blanket that God had me make especially for her. I have to admit, that was incredibly nerve-wracking for a naturally introverted person like me. Who chases someone down to tell them that you think you made a blanket for them because you think God showed you a picture of them in your mind? I do, apparently. I was worried that it would sound a little creepy, but her response was just the opposite. It turns out, she collected blankets. God had just asked her to step down from the worship team so that she could rest. It was an incredibly difficult decision for her to give up something that she loved so much out of obedience to God. And yet, there I was the very last day she was supposed to sing, to meet her with a blanket that represented her favorite place on earth, signifying rest, designed with inspiration from a worship song. God is so cool! Oh, and the pink starfish? That was symbolic for her first grandchild that had just been born, a baby girl. You can't tell me that God isn't in the details.

Sometimes, we try to fit Him into a religious box, convincing ourselves that He's only available to us in certain situations or that He can only help with certain things. Let me just tell you, God is in everything. Quite literally everything. And if we want a limitless life, we have to start inviting Him into a limitless amount of situations. Just try it and see what He can do.

GRATITUDE

Psalms 100:4 says, "Enter his gates with thanksgiving and his courts with praise; give thanks to him and praise his name." This may sound a little contradictory to what I told you before. *I thought you said I could bring Him all of my feelings, now you're telling me to only come to Him with gratitude. Which is it?* The thing is, it doesn't have to be one or the other. If you take a look at a lot of the Psalms David wrote, you'll see that most of them do not start out well. In fact, most of them look pretty grim. The thing is, by the end of the Psalm, David had shifted his focus from his situation to his God.

It is 100% okay to bring God your feelings, I just don't want you to stop there. Don't drain yourself out to Him and then exit the chat. You have to give Him the time to fill you back up. You'll know that He's done that when you leave the conversation full of gratitude and peace. Gratitude is the simple act of shifting your focus. When our focus is only on the problem, we're neglecting to acknowledge the very one who can solve that problem.

When we are able to shift into a heart posture of gratitude, we are basically demonstrating our trust in God. Remember, if you fully trust God, you have complete peace. Anxiety has to bow in the presence of Jesus. It cannot stand in a court of praise. Sometimes, we have to express our gratitude before we ever feel it. If you're anything like me, it can be incredibly tempting to let your feelings guide you. But, I'll tell you the same thing I tell my son all of the time.

> **OUR FEELINGS DON'T BELONG IN THE DRIVER'S SEAT, JESUS DOES.**

If we let our feelings take the wheel, we will likely spend the rest of our lives spinning in circles.

It's important to remember that things happen in the spiritual before we see it in the natural. Kind of like how you can smell food before you ever eat it. As you go along this journey, your "spiritual sense of smell" will heighten and you'll be able to sense what's going on in the spiritual realm before you ever taste it in the natural. This allows you to be able to align yourself with God and be able to call things into existence. If we act according to what we smell God cooking, we will have greater satisfaction when we actually partake of it.

My son has a bad habit of deciding whether he likes a new food or not before he ever tastes it. I have to admit, he gets it honest. I can be the same way at times. There have been times when I have spent a lot of time preparing a meal that I know he will enjoy, only for him to turn his nose up at it because it "looks yucky." There will be times in your life where your situation looks yucky. You'll find yourself looking around you and wondering where God is and how He could possibly be allowing this if He loves you. But if you truly trust God, you'll know that He would never serve you a meal that He knows you wouldn't enjoy. He works everything out for your good, remember? So if things look yucky, He's probably not done cooking yet. Shift your focus from the way things look right now to what you know they can be once God is done with it and you'll find that a posture of gratitude comes naturally, and the peace of God follows as a result.

LEGALISM

When I was growing up, there seemed to be a lot of unwritten rules that you were expected to follow if you loved Jesus. Good Christians should read their Bibles everyday, pray for everyone at all times, be at church every time the doors open, and witness to everyone they see. As a kid, I developed a lot of guilt and shame around that. Because I was a shy child who didn't want to talk to strangers, or who didn't understand the Bible, or who didn't know what to pray, I thought that meant I was following Jesus incorrectly. I was told an awful lot about who Jesus was and what He did during His time on earth, but I never really knew how to pursue a personal relationship with Him. I think that a large part of that was because I was so hyper fixated on trying to follow the rules that I didn't know there was more to it.

Unfortunately, legalism is a door that swings both ways. And as I've grown older and seen people start to develop these personal relationships with Jesus, I've seen that list of unwritten rules start to transition from a list of things Christians should do into a list of things they shouldn't do. For example, now I see people saying that Christians shouldn't read any versions of the Bible except KJV, they shouldn't listen to secular music, shouldn't attend concerts, shouldn't celebrate holidays, and the list goes on. The thing is, a lot of these "rules" are built around other people's convictions, and some of them (not all of them) are good advice for Christians to follow. But it is not your job to follow other people's convictions, nor is it your job to inflict your convictions on other people as if they are laws themselves.

Think about it this way. If you are in poor health, on the verge of diabetes and Jesus offers to show you how to get your health back on track, He may encourage you not to eat chocolate cake. That may be a weakness of yours that He's trying to steer you away from. That doesn't mean that nobody else in the world is allowed to eat chocolate cake because Jesus said so. Do you catch my drift? It may be true that He told you that as it applies to your specific journey with Him, but that doesn't mean that everyone has to adhere to that.

When I was younger, my older brother got a job mowing lawns in the summer. That meant that during those summer months, when my parents had to work, I was responsible for watching my sister who was five years younger than me. I'm sure you've learned by now that I am a rule follower and I take my assignments very seriously, and so I took it upon myself to step into the role of a parent during those hours. My intentions were good. I knew the lessons that my parents had taught me, and they had put me in charge, so I thought it was only logical that I would bestow those same lessons on my sister. It didn't work. In fact, I'm quite certain she wound up resenting me for it. Instead of taking it upon myself to correct her whenever I saw that there was a lesson to be learned, I should have brought it to my parents.

Sometimes we think it's our job as siblings in the body of Christ to correct others based on the lessons God has taught us. It's really tempting, because you just want to see them do well. You don't want to see them make the same mistakes you made. But the whole reason why they are still making those choices is because God either hasn't convicted them of it because it's not applicable to their journey, or they haven't spent enough time in His presence for Him to speak that truth into them. Rather than taking those situations into our own hands, we need to be encouraging them closer to their Father. And if someone is spending all of their time correcting your personal walk with God, consult God about the matter and ask Him if you should regard it as wisdom or disregard it altogether. There is a difference between someone trying to give wise counsel, and trying to bend you to their will. Anyone who is trying to give you wise counsel will be more than willing to talk things out until you can come to a mutual understanding. Anyone who just wants you to follow their rulebook will not entertain another opinion. They may have the best of intentions, but as long as you are in right standing with God, that's all that matters, not what anyone else says.

You see, God is far more concerned about your heart posture rather than your behavior. There have been plenty of innocent things that He has convicted me of all because I was doing them for the wrong reasons. On the other hand, there have been several times where I have asked Him if I could go to a certain place or participate in a certain thing, fully expecting Him to say no because all of the other christians were telling me not to do it. Instead, He asked me, "*Why* do you want to do that? *Why* do you want to go there?" And when I give Him my honest reasons, He tells me He's fine with that. It's not about *what* you're doing, it's about *why* you're doing it. If you're unsure about something, bring it to God. Psalms 37:23 (AMP) says, "The steps of a good and righteous man are directed and established by the Lord." If you have accepted the sacrifice Jesus made for you and made Him Lord of your life, then you are righteous. Allowing God to direct your steps whenever you don't know which way to go keeps you from getting tripped up. By keeping a tight leash on legalism, we keep ourselves free from the trap that it sets.

7

—— · ——

JOURNEY

Now that we've discussed all of the building blocks that led me to pursuing a limitless life with Jesus, I do want to stress the importance of the journey. Our God is a God of process. Oftentimes, we find ourselves struggling with the desire for instant gratification. We want things "quick, fast, and in a hurry" as we say down here in the south. My husband says we live in a "microwave generation" where people want things piping hot in 30 seconds or less. The problem with that is that we serve a crockpot God who likes to slow roast things over low heat. But which one do you think tastes better?

For most of my life, I have had horrible eating habits and, therefore, horrible gut issues. Whenever I would try to make changes to better my health, it seemed like I could never quite stick to them. They were just too difficult to maintain. I had accepted the fact that this was how my body was going to be for the rest of my life — addicted to Dr. Pepper and junk food with horrible bloating and digestion. One day, God randomly asked me if I was ready to kick my Dr. Pepper addiction. I told Him that I was absolutely ready, I had just tried so many times and had so many horrible headaches and withdrawal symptoms that I never could see it through. He said to me, "How about this? You can drink as many Dr. Peppers as you want every day, you just have to drink four bottles of water first." Deal. That seemed so easy. I wasn't limiting myself or following any crazy restrictions, I was just prioritizing what my body needed first. Once I started implementing that simple change, I was in awe of how easy it was to cut soft drinks out of my diet completely. Because my body was getting what it needed, I wasn't craving the sugar and caffeine that soft drinks had to offer. Pretty soon, I quit keeping them in the house. I was amazed that within two months of His suggestion, I had kicked that habit without a single symptom of withdrawal.

After I cut out soft drinks (other than the occasional Dr. Pepper when I'm going out to eat), we tackled my junk food addiction. Then He gave me a strategy to stop snacking as much at night and fueling my body with mostly protein and veggies. After that, I started going to the gym regularly. Before I knew it, a year had gone by and I was in better shape than I had been before I had my babies. I was stronger, healthier, and my digestion had never been better. And it was all because He gave me one simple step of the process at a time. I'm still not quite where I'd like to be, but I have no doubt that He will continue to teach me how to improve my health for as long as I'm in this body. There is no "arriving," the journey is continuous. When you're in the thick of it, it may feel as though things are moving so slowly. You don't want to continue walking through this valley, you want to be on the mountaintop already. But those simple everyday obediences are what get you to the mountaintop.

Imagine being a caterpillar that has to go through the process of turning into a butterfly. In all honesty, a lot of us would probably opt out of that journey if we knew what it would require of us. A caterpillar has to enshroud itself in a cramped cocoon, with only a thin veil to protect it as it turns to absolute goo before completely reassembling into an entirely different creature. Sounds painful, doesn't it? I won't lie to you, at times the process is painful. It's uncomfortable.

> **YOU DON'T BECOME A NEW CREATION WITHOUT THE TRANSFORMATION.**

I think that's worth it, don't you?

REMEMBER THE PROCESS

Sometimes it feels like God moves at a glacial pace when we compare His action to our preferences. We have to remember that we are on a lifelong journey of refinement. You will never get to a point in this lifetime where you have "arrived." You will never learn all there is to learn, grow to the full extent that you can grow, or achieve all that there is to achieve. I realize that that may sound a bit disheartening, but the good news is that you were never designed to do that. We serve an infinite God, which means that we will be learning and growing for the rest of eternity. There will always be new things to discover, new adventures to go on, and more to learn. If you thought that heaven was going to be this boring place where you sit around doing nothing, think again. By pursuing that growth and change here on earth, not only does it make this fallen world easier to bear, but it also gives us a little taste of how God designed everything to be. "Your kingdom come, your will be done, on earth as it is in heaven." (Matthew 6:10). This is how we bring the kingdom of heaven to earth; we relentlessly pursue all that God has for His children.

I do understand that this growth will not always be easy.

> CONSTANT GROWTH MEANS CONSTANT GROWING PAINS.

Adapting and evolving is not always fun. Sometimes it feels like you can't get your footing because everything around you is changing at such a rapid pace. Just remember that you're not expected to build your house on that shifting sand (Matthew 7:24-26). Build your house upon the Rock of Ages, and goodness and mercy will follow you all of the days of your life (Psalm 23:6).

As you start out on this journey, I do want to caution you about one thing. Matthew 7:13-14 says, "Enter through the narrow gate. For wide is the gate and broad is the road that leads to destruction, and many enter through it. But small is the gate and narrow the road that leads to life, and only a few find it." If you are committing your whole life to Jesus, the trek is going to be difficult at times. You are not signing up for a walk in the park, here. If that's what you're after, you can skip on down to that broad and easy path. Just don't be surprised when that path leads you right into a cage. In order to follow along the narrow path, you have to watch your step. You have to continue to follow His ways and walk as He walks. You don't get to a life of limitlessness by cutting corners and taking the easy way out.

Have you ever been hiking? Anyone who hikes on a regular basis can tell you that the best views are the ones that you really have to work for. You don't get an aerial shot by playing along the foothills. You have to commit yourself to climbing that steep incline to get to where you want to go. As long as you're aware of that ahead of time, you can properly prepare and take precautions that would keep you from quitting halfway up the mountain.

I've noticed that a lot of people have a tendency to climb up the wrong mountain. I have seen so many people chasing after all of the fragile things in life that make big promises but never deliver. Things like fame, money, influence and material possessions. They spend their entire lives climbing these mountains only to get to the top and realize that there's nothing but fog. It's kind of like going to the state fair and being lured into a tent that promises to hold a "half spider, half woman hybrid creature." It makes you feel a little dumb that you spent your hard-earned money to see a woman poking her head through a hole in a table surrounded by a halloween spider costume. It's easy to be hooked with empty promises, just not quite as easy to get that hook out of you. Admitting that you have been chasing an empty promise all your life is a hard pill to swallow, and it takes humility to admit that you made a mistake and begin the journey back down that mountain.

In order to pursue everything God has for you, you have to be willing to climb down the mountain that you've built your life on. Now, that doesn't mean that you're trading everything that you've worked for for something of lesser value. Quite the opposite. God has a whole other mountain in store for you. A bigger one with better views and not a cloud in sight once you get to the top. But you can't jump from one mountaintop to the other. Do you remember the story of the rich man who wanted to follow Jesus but wasn't willing to give up his earthly possessions? Jesus said it was easier for a camel to pass through the eye of a needle than it was for a rich man to go to heaven. (Mark 10:25). We can all learn a lesson from that rich young ruler. You have to be willing to scale down that mountain you've been climbing and walk through the valley in order to get to the mountain He had picked out for you in the first place. It's not easy or fun to go through that valley. Thankfully, we have this biblical promise: "Even though I walk through the darkest valley, I will fear no evil, for you are with me" Psalms 23:4. You can rest assured that although the journey will get a little rocky at times, God will be there to guide you every step of the way. He will not leave you in that valley. He will give you every step of the way, one step at a time. All you have to do is keep walking.

I'm sure you've heard the verse "Whoever finds their life will lose it and whoever loses their life for my sake will find it (Matthew 10:39). Losing your life doesn't necessarily mean that you will literally die for Christ. It means that you have to be willing to lay down the ideas of what you thought your life should be in order to fully pursue what He has for you. I once heard Him say to me, "How can I build anything before I know how much material I'm working with?" Clearly, He knows everything, so don't take that statement literally. What I believe He meant was that He has to see how much of myself I'm willing to surrender before He will begin the process of rebuilding my life in the way He intended it to be. I'll let you in on a little secret though: His ways are always better.

My son is about to turn six years old. If I were to give my son the option of planning out his birthday or letting me plan out his birthday, chances are he would want to do it himself so that he could have some form of control over it. It's likely that he would choose to go get ice cream, go to a movie, or some other activity that he doesn't get to do on an average day. And if he chose those things, he could be perfectly happy with those choices. But if he let me, as his parent, plan his birthday, I would make it epic because I know what he likes and I have access to resources that he doesn't have access to. I would be planning things like taking him to Monster Jam or to the aquarium and making a whole trip of it. I would go above and beyond for my child, much further than anything he would dream up for himself simply because I love him. I hope it's starting to sink in by this point that your father loves you. He wants more for your life than you could ever want for yourself, all He needs you to do is trust Him.

SEASONS

Ecclesiastes 3:1(NLT) says, "For everything there is a season, and a time for every activity under heaven." As you go along this journey, you'll likely begin to notice these patterns as they unfold. There will be seasons of waiting and seasons of working, seasons of learning, and seasons to implement what you've learned. Just like the natural seasons that we experience as the weather changes, not all of them will be fun. I don't know anyone who enjoys the winter for extended periods of time. Here in the south, everyone is relieved at first to get a little break from the heat. We enjoy a day or two of snow every handful of years and then we're over it. The thing is, we can't control the seasons. There's nothing that we can do to force the season along or make the weather warm up. You can't force your spiritual seasons to change either.

When I was in elementary school, I remember learning about the cycle of rain. There was a very clear diagram in my science textbook that outlined how water is absorbed into the air through evaporation. Those water droplets then join together to form a cloud, and once that cloud has an abundance of water droplets accumulated, it releases them through precipitation. It seemed like a simple enough concept to me. So simple, in fact, that I thought I could bend the weather to my will. For the next several months, whenever I had an upcoming event that I wasn't looking forward to, I would fill up glasses and jars with water and leave them all over my room so that that water would evaporate into the air, form a rain cloud, and rain out whatever it was that I was avoiding. It seems silly as an adult, and yet, a couple of decades later, I found myself trying to do the same thing with my spiritual seasons.

You see, I thought that breakthrough was completely up to me. I thought that if I just participated and did everything that I needed to do in that season, that I could hurry it along and "change the weather," so to speak. That was, until God gave me a vision one day. In this vision, I was standing in a classroom. With a sledgehammer in hand, I was pounding at the walls trying to break through to the other side. I hear a faint *ahem* behind me and turn to see Jesus standing at a door to the very room I was trying to break into. He opened it ever so gently and stared at me as if to say, "Isn't this easier?" *Oh, that is easier,* I thought to myself. He explained to me, "You think that breakthrough is up to you, but it's not. It's my job to open that door for you whenever you're ready. For now, I just need you to sit down and let me teach you what I need to teach you. We will move on to the next room when it's time." Don't get me wrong, it is incredibly important to participate, but participation is intended to look more like being a student than a construction worker. Just like a teacher in school instructs their students when it's time to move on to the next lesson, we don't get to decide when we're done learning. That's up to God. And we cannot move onto the next season of our lives until we're willing to sit down and be His student.

There will be seasons of drought in your life, seasons of famine, seasons of barrenness, but there will also be seasons of growth, of change, of fruitfulness and of new life.

> DON'T CONFUSE YOUR CURRENT SEASON WITH THE VOLUME
> OF GOD'S LOVE FOR YOU.

God's love is infinite and cannot be measured by our human circumstances. But just like a seed needs to be buried and split open in order to produce growth, these painful seasons will produce more beauty than you could ever imagine. Embrace each season, knowing that it's only going to be there for a designated amount of time.

There was a season of my life where I felt as though I was under constant spiritual warfare. I was in a constant state of learning and adapting, and, honestly, it felt like I was in survival mode most of the time. I was so incredibly ready for that season to be over. I wished it away every day of my life because I constantly felt agitated and stressed. "You're going to miss this," God told me. *Yeah, right,* I thought. And yet when it was time to change seasons and I started seeing the growth of what that season had taught me, I developed a profound gratitude for it. Because although I was under constant attack, I also experienced constant comfort from my Father. When I was in that season, I felt like a newborn baby. I was confused, I didn't know how to communicate what I needed, and sometimes it felt like all I could do was cry out of frustration. And yet when I outgrew that season, I deeply missed the feeling of constantly being held and cared for through my struggles. It's extremely tempting to think that the next season will be better, easier, more fulfilling.

> IF WE DON'T RECOGNIZE EACH SEASON FOR THE BEAUTY
> THAT IT HOLDS, WE WILL WIND UP WISHING OUR LIVES
> AWAY.

So how do you tell what kind of season you're in and when you're moving out of it? One thing that I like to do is find a story in scripture that points to the kind of situation I am currently walking through. Do you feel like the Israelites who had been stripped from everything they had ever known, radically rescued but having to unlearn and relearn the very way you live your life? You may be in a wilderness season. Maybe you are struggling to conceive a baby (whether literally or a figurative dream that's in your heart) and can empathize with Abraham's struggles of waiting for a son for 25 years. You may be in a waiting season. By comparing notes with what's already taken place in scripture, we're able to find guidance on how to handle each season that we're in. When it's time to switch gears and move into the next season, God will tell you. As I've mentioned before, He's going to give you each step, one at a time. If He showed you the whole picture, you would likely be tempted to do it all in your own strength. By only giving us the next step, He makes sure that we remain dependent on His direction. He will begin to drop little clues and confirmations here and there about what you need to do next. All you have to do is remain sensitive to His voice so that you can hear Him when He speaks.

BE PATIENT WITH YOURSELF AND OTHERS

Once you get your first taste of what God has for your life, you're most likely going to reach a point where you want every single person around you to experience the same thing. You might even get frustrated with others because you *know* that if they experience just a fraction of what you've experienced, they would be forever changed too. I'm sure you've heard that old saying, "You can lead a horse to water but you can't make it drink." The same is true with people. You can tell them about all the wonderful things Jesus has done in your life until you're blue in the face, but you cannot *make* them be willing to experience Him. It's a choice that we all have to make out of our own free will.

I understand how frustrating this can be, especially when these people are already Christians, but just aren't digging into the fullness of what God has for them. One day, I found myself extremely frustrated by the way one of the local pastors in our community was handling a situation. I took it to God, complaining about this person. I said, "God, they should know better. They're a pastor, after all." His response was, "So?" God sure does have a habit of keeping me dumbfounded by His answers. "What do you mean, 'so?'" I protested, "They're not representing you well. Doesn't that make you angry?" He responded with the gentleness of a patient parent. "Spiritual growth is a choice. You've watched your kids grow and develop as they've gotten older, but in the spiritual realm, people have to decide that they want to mature. It doesn't happen automatically like physical growth."

Talk about a perspective shift. I had never thought of it that way before. In reality, someone who has been a Christian for 70 years could be on the same maturity level as someone who has been a Christian for 70 days. We all have to decide to mature, and we can't make that decision for other people. But we can use that information to be able to see people the way God sees them.

My son and my daughter have an age gap of almost four years. My son was so patient with his little sister when she was a baby, but as soon as she started learning to crawl and walk and use her fine motor skills, his frustration increased. He would get so angry whenever she would throw things or hit him because he knew that those things were against our family rules. What he didn't understand was that she didn't know any better. She was just a toddler who was learning how to use these skills for the first time. Of course, I knew that she wasn't going to master these things right away. Obviously I didn't want her to hit her brother or throw toys at him, but because of the stage of maturity she was in, I was able to have patience with her as she was learning.

Which person do you resonate with the most in that story? Are you the baby who's just learning new things? Or are you the older brother who is critical of someone who can't follow the rules on the first try? I'd hope that we could all reach a point of maturity where we can see things through the eyes of a loving parent who has patience for both of those children in the stage of life that they are currently in.

We also can't get frustrated with the pace at which each person runs their race. If you are pursuing Jesus, that's what matters. Squash that desire to compare the speed at which your story develops to another person's.

My brother-in-law recently got my son into running for fun. What's fun about running is beyond my understanding, but it's something that they enjoy doing together. During their first race, there was a little boy that my son played soccer with who was also running the race. This kid comes from an extremely athletic family. The whole family was running together. My son wanted so badly to win, but he got second place for his age group. I assured him that it wasn't about the place he came in, it was about finishing the race. If he had let the comparison game get to him that day, it would have robbed him of the joy that he felt just for finishing a race he had never run before. Instead, he accepted that medal with a giant smile on his face and a proud family by his side. The point is that we all have our own race to run. Let's get into the habit of cheering others on as they run, no matter how fast or slow they're going.

As God's children, we all learn things at different times. I've mentioned before that God is an extremely personal God. Most of the time, He caters our experiences to our unique journey with Him. That means that He may reveal things to you in two months that took me two years to learn. That doesn't mean that either of us are pursuing Him incorrectly, it just reinforces the idea that the body of Christ needs each other.

I once heard someone[1] explain it this way: Each person has a different puzzle that they're trying to complete. Rather than giving each person the pieces that they need for their puzzle, God dumps all of the pieces in one big pile for everyone to sort through. Along the way, you may have collected a piece that someone else needs. That's why it's important to share your pieces. Share the things that God has taught you, because it may be the exact thing someone needs to hear to get them through the next leg of their journey.

This is what discipleship is. This is how you share the gospel. Nobody is expecting you to approach a random stranger and ask them if they have the time to discuss our Lord and Savior, Jesus Christ. Just share your puzzle pieces. Bring others along with you as you run the race, just be patient with the pace at which they're moving.

GENERATIONAL CYCLE BREAKERS

For some people, being patient with others can be especially difficult when you are called to go first in your family. Early on in my journey, God told me that I would be "the catalyst for change in my family." Every person in my family has a relationship with Jesus, but He was beginning to teach me lessons that some of them had not yet encountered. At first, I thought that sounded pretty cool, but over time, I started to realize exactly what that meant. It meant that for the majority of those first few years, I felt as though I was fighting a spiritual battle all on my own.

I was given a vision one day of myself in a blizzard. Everyone I loved was standing behind me as I guarded them with my sword drawn. I was the only one with a weapon, and I understood it was my job to protect them and lead them through this storm. The thing is, when you're in a blizzard, you can hardly see your hand in front of your face. I knew I was supposed to be protecting my family from imminent danger, but I didn't understand how to do that when I couldn't even see the danger. I could feel the presence of the enemy all around me, just waiting to attack. I knew we couldn't stay there like a bunch of sitting ducks, so I began to move forward, one step at a time. Every time I would step forward, I would swing my sword, slicing the snowy air in front of me. My family and I began to move forward one small step at a time. Next, I was shown this same vision from a bird's-eye view. I could see myself and my whole family behind me. Just a few feet in front of me seemed to be a mile-long line of darkness, representing the enemy and all of the forces that were against me. Each time I took a step forward and swung my sword, the darkness would back up.

I know that this journey will be especially difficult for you. At times, you will feel as though you are bearing the weight of your family's future all on your own. What I want you to realize is that your family will benefit from your courage. Future generations will be able to look back on their bloodline and discover that you were the one who started this whole revolution that changed the course of history. That may sound a bit excessive, but it's really not. Your role is that important.

This position that you're in may have you feeling vulnerable and uncertain, but I want you to see what a force you are for the kingdom of God. Your very journey is a threat to the principalities of darkness set out to destroy you. The enemy cannot keep you down if you refuse to stay put. The fact that you are moving forward at all means that you have the forces of Satan's army quaking in their boots. Although you may feel weak right now, just remember when Jesus said, "My power is made perfect in weakness" (2 Corinthians 12:9). The times that God's light shines through us the most is when we are chasing down the darkness.

Think of it as your entire family being locked in a jail cell. The generations before you may have just accepted that as the hand that they had been dealt, trying to make the most of a bad situation. As the generational cycle breaker, you are the one who has decided that this prison will no longer be your home. Picking the lock and flinging open those doors won't be easy, but it's necessary in order to set everyone free. Those who come after you will have your obedience to thank for their ability to run free and pursue the ways of God with reckless abandon. Never give up hope for your situation or for your family. I also want you to remember that you don't have to do this in your own power. The latter half of John 14:10 says, "It is the Father, living in me, who is doing his work." God is carrying out His will for your family through your willingness and obedience. All you have to do is continue to listen to His direction.

YOU DON'T HAVE TO FIGURE IT ALL OUT

There was a point in my life where God had asked me to rest. In a season where it felt like there was so much to do, I was confused by His suggestion. I confided in a friend of mine and said, "I just can't figure out why He would ask me to rest right now." Her response was, "Maybe you're not supposed to figure it out." One thing that you can be sure of is that if Satan cannot convince you that you're crazy, his next best option is to try and use your logic against you. He will do his best to convince you that if you cannot figure out the ways of God, they must not be trustworthy. The thing is, our human brains are not meant to understand the things of God. If we could understand everything that God does, that would make Him pretty small and not worth serving. As a good friend of mine likes to say;[2] God is knowable, but God is not figure-out-able. We serve a gigantic God whose ways are incomprehensible to us. Just like children aren't meant to understand every move that their parents make, we are not intended to understand every move that God makes.

Now, there's nothing wrong with seeking answers to the questions in your mind. Just ask yourself why you want to know first. Is it because you want to understand Him better? Or is it because you won't be able to trust Him unless you understand? Those are two very different motivating factors. If we're going to honestly hand our trust over to Him, we have to understand that He's big enough to get us where we need to go exactly when we need to get there. If you're following Him fervently, He's not going to let you miss your exit. Trying to figure things out, in some cases, can counteract placing our trust in Him. Dig deep with your intentions to figure out what your heart posture is, and if you're uncertain, you can always ask Him for help.

Let me close this out by giving you a little peace of mind. You cannot mess up His plans for you, not if you are pursuing Him. Rather than thinking of this journey that you're on as a tightrope where one wrong move will completely knock you off course, think of it more like a choose your own adventure book. Do you remember those books? The concept was that you read a little bit until the character comes to a fork in the road. Then you, as the reader, get to make the choice for that character. The author has written two different outcomes for each choice, along with more and more choices down the line.

He has thought of every scenario and every contingency. Even when you think you've messed everything up, He already saw that mistake coming and found a way to use it. He wastes nothing. Yes, sometimes God has clear cut instructions for your life. Move here, take that job, break up with that person. It's still up to you to choose to listen to Him. At other times, He gives you the options. With the way He's written your book, as long as you are doing your best to follow Him, you'll wind up at your destination either way. The only way you don't get there is by closing the book and refusing to participate. Judging by the fact that you've made it this far, I'd say you're well on your way to discovering the limitless potential that He has for you in this life. Enjoy your journey.

— • —

EPILOGUE

THIS IS JUST THE BEGINNING

It came to me in another vision. I was watching as a wild horse explored the expanse-less terrain at their disposal. Miles and miles of open pastures as far as the eye could see. This horse was running as fast as it could, with power in its legs and freedom in its lungs. After it had been running for a while, this horse came to the base of a mountain. It climbed along the foothills, trying to use its momentum and power to climb higher, but unable to maintain their footing once the mountain wall reached a certain pitch. All of a sudden, an eagle came swooping overhead. Starting in the foothills, it wound its way higher and higher, to the peak of the mountain and beyond.

"This is where I'm taking you," I heard. "What you thought was true freedom was just the beginning. Your potential is absolutely limitless." It was almost as if I could feel the wind rushing through me.

"But God, what exactly are you trying to show me?" I asked. Over the next few weeks, I started seeing eagles everywhere: in real life, in art, in videos. I had the sense He was trying to teach me something, so I began researching eagles. I found that they are at the top of the food chain, having no real dangerous predators that they cannot overcome.

They can fly at altitudes as high as an airplane (up to 20,000 feet above sea level!), meaning that the sky is quite literally the limit for them.

When you're flying that high, there's nothing to bump into, no boundaries to be aware of, and nothing that's able to chase you down. Sure, storms come every now and then, but do you know what an eagle does in a storm? They fly into it and use the air pressure to boost their altitude so that they can fly even higher. It seems as though nothing can touch them. Limitless. This is what is available for me to step into. There is no end to where I can go with God by my side. No ceiling, no finish line, no boundaries. Just me, God, and a lifetime of adventure. The same is available to you, if you're willing to chase after it.

Soar higher, my friend.

ENDNOTES

Hearing God's Voice

1. From *The Candace Cameron Bure Podcast*, Season 2 with Heather MacFadyen

2. Song by country music artist Craig Morgan

Promises

1. From *The Candace Cameron Bure Podcast,* season 4 with Bianca Juarez Olthoff

2. Psalms 37:4, Matthew 7:7 NIV Translation

Identity

1. Pastor Chuck Ford of Relate Church

2. From the teachings of Leif Hetland

3. Shayla Huber, author of *10 Things I Hate About My Husband*

Purpose

1. Pastor Jim Baker of Zion Christian Fellowship, from the "Wealth with God" sermon series

Peace

1. Inspired by teachings from Jennie Allen's podcast, *Made For This*

Intimacy

1. Jenny Donnely, founder of Her Voice

2. Shelby Walls, 48faith_ on Tiktok

Journey

1. Dallas Barbee on Tiktok

2. Shayla Huber, Author of *10 Things I Hate About My Husband*

—— ◆ ——

ABOUT THE AUTHOR

Caitlin Childs is a wife, mother, author and speaker. She is a gifted storyteller who makes even the most difficult concepts easy to understand through the use of analogies and examples. She is passionate about helping people grow one step closer to God by sharing her own personal discoveries and lessons learned along her faith journey.

Connect with Caitlin on social media:
Instagram: @childs.at.heart
Tiktok: @childsatheart

Made in the USA
Columbia, SC
29 January 2024